Three Months with

JOHN

Three Months with

JOHN

Justo L. González

ABINGDON PRESS

Nashville

THREE MONTHS WITH JOHN

Spanish edition copyright © 1998

English translation copyright © 2005 by Abingdon Press

This book is printed on recycled, acid-free, elemental-chlorine–free paper.

Library of Congress Cataloging-in-Publication Data

González, Justo L.
 [Tres meses en la escuela de Juan. English]
 Three months with John / Justo L. González.
  p. cm.
 ISBN 0-687-05714-0 (bdg. : adhesive-perfect : alk. paper)
 1. Bible. N.T. John--Study and teaching. I. Title.

 BS2616.G6613 2005
 226.5'0071--dc22   2004029724

Scripture quotations, unless otherwise indicated, are from the *New Revised Standard Version of the Bible,* Copyright 1989, by the Division of Christian Education of the National Council of the Churches of Christ in the United States of America. Used by permission

05 06 07 08 09 10 11 12 13 14—10 9 8 7 6 5 4 3 2 1

MANUFACTURED IN THE UNITED STATES OF AMERICA

C O N T E N T S

INTRODUCTION

This book is an invitation to study and to adventure. As a study it will require discipline. As an adventure, it will offer new panoramas and exciting challenges.

Let us address discipline. Every important goal in life requires a discipline. If a young person wishes to become, for instance, a doctor or a lawyer, it will be necessary to follow from an early age a discipline of study and learning. If we are concerned about our physical health, we try to follow a discipline of exercise and nutrition. Athletes who prepare to compete in the Olympics must subject themselves to a rigid discipline for years on end. And yet, when it comes to spiritual life, very few Christians are willing to subject themselves to a discipline that will develop and strengthen it. With the excuse that we should "pray without ceasing," we do not set aside a particular time for prayer. And, since the Bible is always there, ready to be opened and read whenever we need it, we do not set a program of study. The result is that both our prayer and our knowledge of the Bible suffer, just as the body suffers when instead of following an ordered diet and a discipline of exercise we eat whatever strikes our fancy and exercise only when we feel like it.

The first thing that we need in order to develop a discipline of study is to set aside a time and a place. The studies in this book follow a weekly rhythm: Each week there will be six short studies and a longer one. If you then follow this study privately, you will require at least half an hour a day for the six short studies and an hour for the longer one. Consider your weekly calendar and decide the best time for you to set aside for study. Once you have done this, make every possible effort to fulfill that commitment. Little by little, just as it happens with physical exercise, that study rhythm will become more and more important for you, and the time will come when, if for some reason you are not able to follow it, you will feel the need for it.

If you are using this book as part of a Bible study group that gathers once a week, establish your rhythm of study so that the six shorter sessions take place on the days that you study in private, and the longer one on the day the group meets.

On the other hand, don't be too idealistic regarding the time you have set aside for study. Life always has its unexpected interruptions, and therefore very few people are able to follow a discipline of study without interruption. Sooner or later the day will come when it will be impossible for you to study during the time that you have set aside. In that case, do not be disheartened. That very day, even if at another time, try to study the material assigned for it.

A place for study is almost as important as a time. To the extent possible, have a particular place where you normally do your private study. This will help you avoid distractions. It will also be a convenient place for you to keep your Bible, this book, your notebook of personal reflections, and any other material that you may find useful.

The next important point in developing a discipline of Bible study is the method one follows. There are many good methods for the study of Scripture. The one that we shall follow in this book consists of three fundamental steps: **See**, **Judge**, and **Act**.

However, before we discuss these three steps, there are two important elements that must be stressed, without which no Bible study can be productive: prayer and reflection.

At the very moment you begin each study, approach God in prayer. Ask that the Holy Spirit be with you during this study, helping you understand God's Word, and that the Spirit remain with you after you have completed the session, helping you to follow what you have decided. Always remember that, even though you seem to be by yourself, you are not alone; God is right there with you. It is not just a matter of you and your Bible, but rather of you, your Bible, and the Holy Spirit.

After a few minutes of prayer, devote some time to reflection, reviewing what you have studied before. In particular, remember those decisions you have made on previous days. Read your notebook. Evaluate what you have accomplished. Ask God for the strength to go forward.

Move then to the three steps of **seeing, judging,** and **acting.** As you will note, the material offered under each study is organized according to those three steps. The first, **seeing,** consists in examining the situation before you. In the case of these Bible studies, seeing will involve examining the passage itself. What does it say? Why does it say it? Who are the main characters? What role do they play in the text? What is the context of what is said? In this first stage, we are not asking what the text might mean for ourselves, or what it requires of us. We are only trying to understand the passage itself.

The second step, **judging,** consists of asking ourselves what the text might mean for us. Here, our personal experiences and our concrete situation become very important. We read the Bible in the light of those experiences and that situation, and ask what the Bible says about them. Therefore, when this book invites you to judge, it does not mean for us to judge the biblical text, but rather to invite the text to help us judge our own life, situation, opportunities, and responsibilities. What does the text tell us about the church, about our faith, about our society? How does it affirm and support what we are doing and what we are? How does it question or correct it? What does the text call us to do or to be?

These first two steps lead to the third: **acting.** What we have seen in the biblical text, and the manner in which we judge that text refers to our reality, requires that we act in a specific manner. We do not study the Bible out of curiosity, but in order to be more obedient to God's will. Therefore, the process is incomplete if we are content with seeing and judging. If we are to be obedient, we must act.

Acting can take many diverse forms, depending both on the text and on our own situation. For instance, the study of a certain passage may lead us to greater commitment to the poor and the needy in our community. The study of another passage may call us to witness to our fellow workers. And a third passage may call us to greater faithfulness in our participation in Christian worship. Furthermore, acting does not always imply physical activity. In some cases, acting may consist in a further prayer of repentance. In other cases, it may be abandoning a prejudice we have. Sometimes the action to be taken may be very concrete and brief; for instance, calling someone whom we may have offended. In other cases, it may be a long-term decision; for instance, taking up a different career. But what is always true is that, if we really study the Bible in a spirit of obedience, the Word that comes from God's mouth will not return empty, but will accomplish that for which it was sent (Isaiah 55:11).

Sometimes you will find that there are more suggestions for action than you can possibly follow. Take them simply as what they are: suggestions. Don't feel compelled to do whatever the book suggests. But do feel compelled to respond to your study of the Bible by an act of obedience—whatever that may be.

It is important to remember that we do not read and study the Bible only to be *informed*, but also and above all to be *formed*. We do not read the Bible so much to learn something, as we read it to allow that something to shape our lives. Once again, the example of physical exercise fits the case. Whoever exercises, lifts weights not only to see how much she or he can lift (in order to be *informed*), but also, above all, to become stronger, to be able to lift greater weight (that is, to be *formed*). Likewise, our purpose in these Bible studies should be not only to learn something, to know the Bible better, but also to allow the Bible to shape us, to make us more in accord with the will of our Creator.

This implies that the method of **seeing, judging,** and **acting** should be more like a circle than like a straight line. What this means is that acting improves our seeing, so that in fact the method could be described as seeing, judging, acting, seeing, judging, acting, seeing, and so forth. Every Bible study that we complete, each action that we take, will make us better able to move on to the next study. In order to understand this, think about a traveler in a valley. In that valley, the traveler sees a dense forest, a road that climbs a hill, and the position of the sun. On the basis of what he **sees**, the traveler **judges** that he is not to try crossing the forest, but rather to follow the road. He also **judges**, on the basis of the position of the sun, in which direction he should go. Then he **acts**; he begins walking. Eventually he finds himself atop the hill, where he **sees** new views that allow him to **judge** the direction to be followed and invite him to **act** in a way that he could not have guessed when he was in the valley. Therefore, his **acting** took him to a new way of **seeing**. The same will be true in a Bible study. If we make progress, we shall see ever wider views, and therefore not only will our seeing and judging lead us to a more faithful acting, but also our acting will clarify our seeing and judging.

What resources will you need to follow these studies? First of all, the Bible itself. Sometimes you will be tempted to shorten the time of study by not reading the Bible, and reading only what this book says. The temptation will be even greater when the biblical passage is well known. It is important to resist that temptation. The purpose of this book is to help you in your study of the Bible, not to be a substitute for it. In the studies that follow, the Bible is quoted according to the New Revised Standard Version (NRSV). Therefore, if you use that version it will be easier to follow these studies. Naturally, if you have more time, you may wish to compare different versions to enrich your study. Some people following these studies have reported that they have used a Bible with large letters and wide margins, so that they could write notes and comments. That is up to you.

Second, use this book. Try to follow the rhythm of studies suggested, reading and studying each passage on the day assigned. We are too used to living life in a hurry. Instead of cooking a roast for five hours, we place it in the microwave for thirty minutes. Sometimes we want to do the same with our spiritual life. If it is good for us to do one of these Bible studies a day, why not go ahead and do them all at once? Here once again the example of physical exercise may be useful. If you try to do a month's worth of exercise in a single day, the results will be very different than if you establish a rhythm of exercise and stick to it. Likewise, if we wish the Bible to shape us, to strengthen and to nourish our spiritual life, it is necessary for us to establish a rhythm that we can continue in the long run.

Third, you will need a notebook in which to write down your reflections, resolutions, and experiences. Write in it, not only what is suggested in some of the studies in this book, but also anything that seems relevant to you. If something strikes your interest, but you cannot follow up on it at the time, make a note of it. Write your answers to the questions posed in the book. Make a note of your decisions, your doubts, your achievements, your failures. Use it at the beginning of each study session, in the period set aside for reflection, in order to help you to remember what you have learned and thought in the course of your three months of study of the Gospel of John.

Make sure that every time you begin a study session you have at hand all of these resources: your Bible, this book, your notebook, and a pencil or pen.

No other resources are absolutely necessary for these studies. But if you wish to study the Gospel of John more deeply, there are other tools that you may find useful: (1) several versions of the Bible, in case you want to compare them; (2) a good commentary on John; (3) a dictionary of the Bible; (4) a biblical atlas. These resources will be particularly helpful if the seventh session of each week will be a group study, and you are responsible for leading the group.

Finally, do not forget two resources readily available to you that are absolutely indispensable for any good Bible study. The first is your own experience. Some of us have been told that when we study the Bible we should leave aside all our other concerns. Nothing could be further from the truth. The Bible is here to respond to our concerns, and therefore our experience and our situation in life help us to understand the Bible and to hear God's Word for us today.

The second such resource is the community of faith. I have already pointed out that when you study the Bible you are not alone with your Bible; but the Holy Spirit of God is also there.

Now I must add that, in a very real sense, your faith community is also there. The Gospel of John was probably written to be read out loud, in the gathering of the church. Therefore, when you read it, even though you may be alone, keep in mind the community of faith that surrounds and upholds you. Read it not only as God's Word for you, but also as God's Word for the church. That is why this book includes the longer Bible study each week: to encourage readers to use it in study groups. These groups may gather once a week, but during the other six days you will each know that the rest of the group is studying the same Bible passage.

I said at the beginning of this introduction that this book is an invitation both to study and to adventure. On this last point, it is best to say no more. Adventures are best when they are unexpected and surprising. Plunge then into the study of the Gospel of John, knowing that at some point it will surprise you, but knowing and trusting also that, even in such surprises, God is already there ahead of you, waiting for you with open arms!

A Word on John

The Gospel of John is different from the other three Gospels, which are jointly called the Synoptic Gospels. The Synoptic Gospels depict the ministry of Jesus as taking place mostly in Galilee, and culminating with the last few days in Jerusalem. In John, Jesus moves back and forth between Galilee and Jerusalem, generally finding much more support in Galilee than in Jerusalem, and having a protracted conflict with the religious leadership in Jerusalem. In any case, John seems to be much less interested in the chronology of events—which is a particular concern of Luke—and much more in their meaning for Christian faith. For this reason, it is often said that John is "more philosophical" than the Synoptics. And for this reason also, many have thought that the background of this Gospel is to be found in Greek philosophical thought—some even claiming that it was written fairly late, at some point in the second century.

Recent scholarship and discoveries, however, correct these

opinions at least on two points. First, as to the date of composition, we now know that the Gospel of John was already circulating in the last decades of the first century. Second, as to the milieu in which it was formed, scholarly consensus is now inclined to think that this book originated in a Christian community that was still mostly Jewish, and which was struggling with their own expulsion from the synagogues and from Jewish community life in general. Thus the anonymous author of this book—whom we shall continue calling "John" in deference to long-standing tradition—was most probably a Christian Jew, who wrote his book sometime about A.D. 90. (Although there are points of contact and similarities among the Gospel of John, the Epistles of John, and the Revelation of John, stylistic and other considerations would seem to indicate that these three bodies of literature, while having some connections as to the milieu in which they arose, were not written by the same person.)

A final note may be helpful as you study the Gospel of John. Quite probably this book was written to be read in worship, just before the celebration of communion, as a way to help worshipers come to a fuller understanding of the Gospel and its significance for their own lives. Thus, John's interests are liturgical and pastoral, rather than historical or biographical. The stories are not framed and ordered as in a biography. They are intended rather to help the reader experience and understand the presence of Jesus in worship and in daily life—and the connection between the two. As you now spend the coming three months with John, it is my hope and prayer that you too may come to experience a closer connection between your life of worship and your daily life.

W E E K

ONE

First Day: Read John 1:1-13.

See: If we compare the Gospel of John with the other three Gospels, we will note that John's is the only one that begins by placing the coming of Jesus within the context of all of creation. Mark begins with the preaching of John the Baptist. Matthew opens with a genealogy that places Jesus within the history of Israel. Luke opens his story by placing it within the framework of the political history of the times, telling us who was in power when Jesus was born; and he then includes a genealogy that goes as far back as Adam, thus making Jesus the culmination of all human history. But only John goes back to the very beginning of all things, claiming "all things came into being through him."

This tells us that the Gospel of John will have cosmic dimensions. Even while placing Jesus firmly within the context of the history of Israel (like Matthew), and within the context of the history of all humankind (like Luke), John's frame of reference will be wider still: "all things." There is nothing that is totally unrelated to the message of the gospel—from the smallest grain of sand to the most distant star. This Word about whom we will learn in John's book is such that "all things came into being through him, and without him not one thing came into being."

This is why verse 11 tells us "he came to what was his own." Jesus did not come into an alien world. He did come to a world that was estranged from God; but not to an alien world, for this world was created through the Word that was made flesh in Jesus. This message is at the very center of the Gospel of John: Jesus comes to save a world that is really his, but that does not wish to acknowledge him.

Judge: There has always been a tendency among Christians to think that some things are of God, and others are not. In some extreme cases, there are those who believe that "spiritual" reality has to do with God, but not the rest of reality. Thus, some Christians have thought that enjoying the beauty of the physical world—flowers, animals, stars—draws us away from the contemplation of God and of spiritual reality.

Even though in most of our churches we do not find such extreme "spiritualism," there are milder versions of the same attitude. Thus there are some who think that true believers must listen only to a certain kind of music—music that has been traditionally associated with the Christian faith—and that all other music must be eschewed. There is no doubt that there are some contemporary songs whose words are blasphemous, and which therefore show once more the rebellion of the world against its Maker. But this does not mean that all nonreligious music is bad and draws us away from God. The sense of hearing, musical notes, and an aesthetic sense are all part of God's creation, made through the same Word who came to us in Jesus Christ. If we reject all of this, we are also rejecting its Creator.

If "all things" were made through him, there is no "thing" that is bad in itself. There are bad uses, bad habits, bad actions. But nothing is evil in and of itself, as it was made and intended through the Word.

Act: Pray: "During these weeks, Lord, help me discern and celebrate your creative hand in all the things you have made. Teach me not to reject or condemn anything or anyone in this creation of yours. Help me distinguish between the good things you have made, and the evil use to which we humans put your good creation. I pray in the name of Jesus Christ, the Word through whom all things were made. Amen."

Second Day: Read John 1:14.

See: This verse is at the very heart of John's message. Much had been written before John about the Word—most of it by pagan writers and philosophers. It was commonly held that the Word is the divine principle that is the source of all reality and all knowledge. Therefore, most of what we read yesterday about the Word, how all things were made through him, and how he is the light that illumines all humankind, may be found in other ancient writings. What is radically new, what pagan writers never dared claim, is that "the Word became flesh and lived among us."

This radical claim that God became flesh is important for several reasons. Consider two of them briefly: The first is that what Christianity proclaims is not a series of abstract doctrines. Even though some have thought otherwise, Christianity is not a set of doctrines or even a set of moral principles. Christianity is no less and no more than the very fact of Jesus Christ—the fact that the eternal Word of God, through whom all things were made, was made flesh and dwelt among us. In order to be a Christian believer, the crucial point is not in accepting a particular doctrine, nor in following a particular way of life, but in meeting Jesus, this incarnate Word who dwelt and still dwells among us.

Second, this is important because it tells us that flesh, the body, and physical matter are important. The Word was not ashamed of taking human flesh. Therefore, his followers must never look upon the body or physical reality as something evil or negative.

Judge: One of the many things that the Word made and that sometimes we tend to consider evil is the body. Throughout the history of the church there have often been those who have thought that holiness consists in ignoring the body, in acting as though it did not exist, and even in punishing it. Sometimes we even imagine that the reason why we sin is that we have bodies.

By thinking this way we blame God for our sin, for God is our creator and the maker of our bodies. However, sin is the result of our willful rebellion against God. It is because of our rebellion that we use the body for sin. Likewise, because of the same rebellion we also sin with our minds and with all of our faculties.

In itself, the body is good. It is good because God created it.

Upon taking human flesh the eternal Word of God confirmed its goodness. How is our church a sign that the body is good, and that God loves it? How do you show that the body is God's good creation?

Act: Resolve to take good care of your body, as well as of the bodies of others. Adjust your diet to make it healthier and set for yourself an exercise program. This too is serving the God who made the body. As for the bodies of others, seek ways to help those who need food, clothing, or shelter. If such a program does not exist in your church, discuss it with others, so that your church may develop programs showing that it too, together with its Lord and Creator, is concerned for the well-being of human bodies.

Third Day: Read John 1:15-28.

See: These verses tell part of the story of John the Baptist. The Gospel tells us that John the Baptist was sent by God. It also tells us that he was not sent to speak about himself, but to point to Jesus. This is told in the first chapter of John at least three times: First, in John 1:8-9, where we are told that John was not the light but was to give witness to the light. Second, it appears in the conversation between John and the messengers sent by some Jewish leaders, where John declares that he is not the Christ (1:20). Third, it appears again in 1:23, where John is a voice preparing the way of the Lord.

The story is straightforward. John began preaching and some from among the religious leadership came to ask him who he was, by which they meant by what authority he was preaching. John answered that he was not preaching about himself but about the one who was to come. We are not told whether John's interlocutors returned to Jerusalem immediately, or were still there on the following day when the story continues. The important point is that John makes it very clear that, no matter how great he may seem, he is much less than the one who comes after him.

Judge: John's focus on Jesus is important, for one of the most common problems for Christians is how to give a witness in such a way that if focuses attention on Jesus, and not on us. An example may help us understand this point. Suppose that we stand at a crossroads, where a sign tells us which way leads to a certain city. That sign has to be sufficiently large and clear so it may be seen by those who pass by. If it is too small, or if it is covered by undergrowth, travelers will miss it, and it will be useless. Also, the sign must somehow relate to the city itself. In our society, this is usually the name of the city. But in societies where there is a high illiteracy rate the sign may be a painting of a salient point, or of a famous building in the city. If the sign has the wrong name, it will point us in the wrong direction, and we will lose the way. Likewise, if the city where we want to go is famous for its beaches, a drawing of a city on top of a mountain will not be much help. The sign has to point to the city, and to represent it faithfully.

However, it is also important to remember that the sign points to the city, but is not the city. If the sign is painted in such a way that when we see a picture of the city we think we have arrived, it will be of no help, for it too will confuse us and cause us to be lost.

Something similar happens with John the Baptist, and also with us. In order for us to be true witnesses to Jesus Christ, there must be something in our lives that points to him, so that those who see and hear us see and hear something of Jesus. As in the case of a sign by the road, others must be able to read the name of Jesus in us. Without this, our witness does not have much value—like a sign that bears a name but points in the wrong direction.

But we must also be careful to make it clear, both to ourselves and to others, that the sign is not the reality. We simply point to Jesus. If we find people admiring us rather than Jesus, we would be like a sign that instead of pointing to a city tries to pass for the city itself.

Can you think of cases when your witness (or that of the church) has lost power because people could not see in you (or in the church) the name of Jesus? Can you think of cases when a supposed witness to Jesus Christ has centered on the witness rather than on Jesus himself?

Act: Write down your answers to these questions. Consider ways in which your life and your witness could point to Jesus more truthfully and effectively. Ask this, not only about yourself, but also about your entire community of faith. Share these thoughts with at least one other person.

Fourth Day: Read John 1:29-34.

See: It was on the next day that John gave witness to the Christ, no longer speaking about one who was to come, but actually pointing to Jesus. In verse 29 John sees Jesus coming and says: "Here is the Lamb of God who takes away the sin of the world." Up to this point, John had said only that he was preparing the way for the Promised One. Now he points at a particular person, Jesus, and says, "he is the one."

John then insists that Jesus is much more than John himself. Although Jesus came after John, in truth he was first. The passage ends with the testimony of John the Baptist that it is only by the Holy Spirit whom he saw descend upon Jesus that he knew that this was the promised Messiah (1:31-33).

Twice (verses 31 and 33) John says that he did not know Jesus. This does not mean that he did not know him in the sense of never having seen him. Luke tells us that they were related. It means rather that John did not know that Jesus was the Christ. John has been sent to announce that the Christ is about to come. He is faithful to that mission and he announces the coming of the Christ. When the commission sent by the religious leaders from Jerusalem asks him about this, he answers that he is indeed announcing the coming of the Messiah. He does not tell them who the Messiah is, because it is only the next day that he recognizes Jesus as such.

Judge: John's announcement of the coming Messiah reminds us that it is not necessary to have all the answers in order to speak in God's name. We sometimes imagine that before witnessing to Jesus we must know much, in order to have a response to any question asked. The truth is that on these matters we will never know so much that we do not have a great deal to learn. To give witness to Jesus, one does not have to know everything. It is a matter not of knowing, but of obeying.

Think again about the case of a road sign. The sign points to a city that is several million times larger than the sign itself. For the sign to be useful it does not have to include every detail about the city. It only has to be in the proper place, and point in the right direction. The same is true of John the Baptist. For him to give witness to Jesus, he does not need to know exactly how God will fulfill what has been promised. It suffices for him to be obedient to what he already knows and to announce it.

God also calls us to give witness, not to a messiah who is about to come, but to one who has already come and who will come again. On that score, we have an advantage over John the Baptist. And yet too often, in spite of such an advantage, we do not bear witness, often hiding behind the excuse that we do not know enough. In this case, perhaps what we ought to do is to give witness to what we already know, while also seeking to learn more.

John Wesley tells of a time when he told a friend that he did not dare preach salvation, because he was not certain of having attained it. The friend suggested that, as he continued seeking salvation, he should continue preaching it in the knowledge that it did exist; and that after finding it, he should then preach it even more earnestly, precisely because he had found it. Shortly afterward, Wesley did receive assurance of his salvation, feeling his "heart strangely warmed" as a passage about Romans written by Martin Luther was read at a meeting he was attending near Aldersgate Street in London. Do you think Wesley's friend gave him good advice?

Act: Resolve to bear witness to Jesus to at least one other person in the next twenty-four hours. Tomorrow, as you begin your daily Bible study, write the result in your notebook.

Fifth Day: Read John 1:35-42.

See: As in yesterday's passage, John the Baptist calls Jesus "the Lamb of God." This is a phrase that does not appear elsewhere in the New Testament—although the book of Revelation does speak of Jesus as "the Lamb." Readers steeped in the traditions of the Hebrew Bible would immediately think of Genesis 22, where Abraham was taking Isaac to be sacrificed. Isaac asked his father where the lamb was for the sacrifice, and Abraham answered that God would provide it. Thus, in referring to Jesus as the Lamb of God, John the Baptist appears to be announcing that Jesus will stand in as a sacrifice in the believers' stead, just as God provided a lamb to be sacrificed instead of Isaac.

The same phrase would also bring to mind the story of Exodus 12, when Moses told the people of Israel that each family should sacrifice a lamb and mark their door with the blood of the lamb, so that the angel of death sent against the firstborn of Egypt would pass over their homes. Thus, the title "Lamb of God" would lead readers to remember that believers, like those ancient doorposts, are sealed for salvation with the blood of this Lamb.

The passage also tells us that Jesus gave Simon a new name, Peter. In the other Gospels we are told that Jesus gave this name to Simon in connection with Simon's declaration that Jesus was the Messiah. This renaming was so important in the life of Simon that throughout history, and to this day, Simon has been known by his new name—"Cephas" in Aramaic and "Petros" in Greek, both meaning "Rock."

Judge: Names are very important. This is why when we have a child we give the matter of naming so much thought. In today's passage we see this in two cases. First is Jesus himself, whom John the Baptist calls "the Lamb of God." That name itself tells us much about who Jesus is and what he is to do. As the lamb was sacrificed in Egypt to save the people of God, so will Jesus, the Lamb of God, be sacrificed for the salvation of his people.

The other case is Simon, whom Jesus renames "Cephas" or "Peter," and who will eventually be known, not as "Saint Simon," but as "Saint Peter." Although John does not say why Jesus gave him this new name, or what was its significance, the fact is that in a way every disciple of Jesus—including us—

Sermon (handwritten marginalia)

receives a <u>new name</u>. This may not take the form of having a new "handle," but it certainly implies becoming a new person. It is impossible to accept the lordship of Jesus and to devote one's life to him without becoming a new person. This is just another way of saying what John will tell us in chapter 3 about being born again.

Act: Write you own name in your notebook. If you know its meaning, write that down too. Now think about your own life as a disciple of Jesus and imagine a name that would help you remember what you ought to be. For instance, if you know that you are a born pessimist, with a tendency to dejection and despair, that name could be "Hope." The word you choose does not have to be an actual name, as long as it tells you something about a goal that you should seek in your Christian life. It could be "Loving," or "Humble," or "Helpful," or "Firm," or "Understanding"—any word that will serve as a reminder of your goal. Think about that word, and about what you could do right now to be true to this hidden name. Write it on a small piece of paper or a small card and put it in your wallet. From now on, whenever you see that paper, let it call you to greater obedience.

Devote de (handwritten marginalia)
Faithful (handwritten marginalia)
antexoual (handwritten marginalia)

Sixth Day: Read John 1:43-51.

See: Today we are studying the calling of two other disciples, Philip and Nathanael. John tells us that Philip was from Bethsaida, a town in Galilee where Jesus visited frequently. Although John does not say where Nathanael is from, he later tells us that Nathanael was from Cana, another town in Galilee where tomorrow's narrative will take place.

John tells us very little about Philip's calling. Jesus goes to Galilee and tells Philip, who was from that area, to follow him. About Nathanael's calling we are given a bit more information. Nathanael was <u>skeptical</u> about what Philip was telling him about Jesus, for he found it difficult to believe that anything good could come out of Nazareth, much less the Messiah. Jesus convinces him through a miracle, telling Nathanael that he had seen him under a fig tree even before Philip went to see him. In response, Nathanael declares him to be the Son of God and King of Israel—in other words, he now accepts what he refused to believe when Philip told him.

Jesus tells him that Nathanael was wrong to wait to see a miracle before he would believe, but also promises that he will see many more miracles.

Judge: It is interesting to note that Nathanael, who came from the small village of Cana, looks down upon neighboring Nazareth, which although still a small town, was much larger than his own Cana. What we see here is that Nathanael, himself a Galilean, is convinced that the center of God's action is Jerusalem, and that it is therefore from Jerusalem, and not from Nazareth or any other place in Galilee, that the Messiah will come.

But there is more. Among Jews, Galilee was considered to be an outcast region—to the point that it was often called "Galilee of the Gentiles" (Isaiah 9:1; Matthew 4:15). Galilee was located far out on the northern fringes of the Holy Land, and was separated from Judea by Samaria. Thus, although Galileans thought of themselves as Jews and certainly not as Gentiles or Samaritans, the "true" Jews from Judea considered them second-class Jews. (That is why in the Gospels, when we often find references to "the Jews," what is in fact meant is the Judeans, or even in many cases the leading Judeans in Jerusalem.)

This means that in this passage a Galilean, whom the Jews from Judea—from the center of power and religion—would consider a second-rate Jew, himself accepts such prejudice, and declares that nothing good can come from Nazareth—that is to say, from a neighboring town in Galilee. In brief, this Galilean echoes the prejudices against his own people.

Quite often, prejudice is so powerful that it convinces, not only those who think of themselves as superior or better, but even those against whom others are prejudiced. In some ways, this is the most insidious power of prejudice. Not only does it close doors and opportunities for those who are excluded, but it also enters the minds of the excluded, convincing them, at least in part, that perhaps there is good reason for their exclusion.

Nathanael believes that the Judeans from Jerusalem are right, and that nothing good will come out of his own people.

Act: Consider some of the prejudices prevalent in our society—and often even in the church. How are you involved in them? Are you prejudiced against someone? Is someone prejudiced against you? Do you find it difficult to recognize the value and promise in some people, either because they belong to a group or class of people from which you do not expect much, or because they are so well known to you that you cannot see their possibilities? Ask yourself, what good can come out of my own neighborhood and community? Write down your reflections.

Seventh Day: Read John 2:1-12.

See: Today's passage is one of the first miracles of Jesus mentioned in the Gospel of John. Note that John says that this happened "on the third day." If we begin counting from the day on which John the Baptist received the delegation of religious leaders and announced the coming of the Messiah, we shall see that the Gospel of John places within a single week all the events that we too have studied in a week. Since in the other Gospels there is more time between these various events, many scholars suggest that the Gospel of John has liturgical purposes—that is, that it does not seek to tell the life of Jesus in a strict chronological order, as Luke and others do, but rather tells it following an order and a rhythm similar to the manner in which the church experiences its relationship to Jesus in its life and worship. In the ancient church, long before there was a Christian year (Advent, Christmas, Easter, Pentecost, etc.), there was a Christian week that set the rhythm for devotion and worship. Therefore, it is possible that the reason why John begins his Gospel by placing all events within a week is that he expected his book to be read and discussed in a worship setting.

Notice that Jesus is not very willing to perform this miracle. He is only one of the many guests at the wedding feast. When his mother suggests that he perform the miracle, Jesus tells her that his "hour" has not yet come. This theme of the "hour" of

Jesus appears repeatedly in the Gospel of John. It is not simply the time of his victory, but is also the time of his suffering, followed by resurrection and renewed life. Jesus' hour will come when the leaders of the people, seeing his miracles and hearing his teachings, will decide that he must be destroyed. That is why Jesus would rather not perform the miracle. He does not wish to hasten his hour.

But his mother insists, and finally Jesus responds to the need of the moment. The need for more wine is not a matter of life and death. It is not the case of a father who has lost his daughter as elsewhere in the Gospels. It is not even the case of a lame man who cannot walk or a blind man who cannot see. It is simply a party that may go awry for lack of wine. It is a recently wedded couple that will be shamed for not having enough for their guests. And yet Jesus responds to this need, which is minuscule when compared to the tragedies of the world or the eternal destiny of souls. Furthermore, Jesus responds with abundance and quality. What he produces is six jars full of wine, each holding twenty or thirty gallons, that is, between a hundred and twenty and a hundred and eighty gallons of wine! And this wine is of such quality that the steward asks the groom why he reserved the better wine for the end rather than serving it first as was customary.

Judge: A very common problem for those of us who seek to understand and follow Jesus is that sometimes we are far too serious. We imagine that God being God, only the more serious matters of life are of divine concern. There have been Christians who have thought that laughter is a sin, and that matters such as art and music have no place in the Christian life. Without going so far, there are also many who think that only what is of transcendental significance and of utmost seriousness should occupy the attention of a disciple. The result is long-faced and embittered believers who spend too much time criticizing those who seem to have too much fun.

But in this passage Jesus shows that such attitudes are contrary to his spirit. Jesus goes to the wedding feast, not necessarily to preach to those present nor to dampen or moderate the festivities, but simply to join the party. And when the scarcity of wine threatens to "rain on the parade," Jesus takes water and turns it into wine. Those of us who would prefer a more austere master may not like it. But this is the Jesus of the Gospels.

Think of yourself and your church. When people look at you, will they be led to think that Jesus is a Lord of joy and celebration? Or will they think rather that Jesus is a killjoy who does not want people to enjoy life or to celebrate important occasions? How can you make sure that your witness is serious and responsible and yet joyful and jovial?

Act: Review your actions and attitudes this past week. Did you scowl or criticize someone else's joy, thinking that in so doing you were witnessing to the faith? Were you a witness, not only to dedication and piety, but also to Christian joy? Write down your reflections. Resolve that during this coming week you will seek to show others that your faith is one of joy and celebration.

For Group Study

After studying and discussing the passage, point out that Jesus took the jars that were set aside for the religious rites of purification. He had them filled with water and turned it into wine. Now there is no jar for purification. Ask the following questions and lead the group in a discussion:

1) What will happen if some people come to be purified?

2) Can we think of any similar situations in the life of the church today?

W E E K
TWO

First Day: Read John 2:13-25.

See: John does not say how long after the events of the first chapter the cleansing of the Temple took place. The other Gospels place this event much later in the ministry of Jesus. Once again, it seems that John is ordering his narrative in order to serve the purposes of reading in the church, rather than in a simple chronological order. All we are told is that the feast of Passover was approaching. This celebration reminded Israel of the time when the angel of death passed over the Hebrew homes, which were marked with the blood of the lamb, and entered the homes of the Egyptians killing their firstborn.

John says that Jesus "went up" to Jerusalem because the city was in fact in a high place, and reaching it from the rest of Judea required climbing up to it.

Those whom Jesus found in the Temple were not ordinary merchants. Their function was to provide animals and other goods for ritual sacrifices. Since it was required that anything offered to God in sacrifice must be pure and perfect, it had become customary for the priesthood to certify it as such. This resulted in a business collaboration between priests and merchants that often led to exploitation of the people, since goods certified as apt for sacrifice were sold at a much higher price than normal. When in verse 18 John refers to those who questioned Jesus' authority as "the Jews," he is actually referring to people from Judea—that is, to Judeans. In other words, what is happening is that those in authority in Jerusalem are questioning the authority of this meddlesome Galilean to disturb life in the Temple.

We are then told that Jesus responded by referring to his own resurrection, but those who had questioned him thought he was speaking of the Temple. You will remember that one of the accusations against Jesus and his early disciples (for instance, against Stephen in Acts 6) was that they blasphemed against the Temple. Thus John is beginning to set the stage for the enmity of the Judean leadership against Jesus and his Galilean band.

Judge: In contrast to yesterday's scripture, where we saw Jesus rejoicing at a wedding and even improving the celebration by turning water into wine, today we see him railing against those who have turned the faith of the people into a means of exploitation. Jesus certainly knows how to celebrate life, but he is also actively and strongly opposed to those who misuse religion. In this case, his opposition is to those who enrich themselves by using the desire of people to offer worthy and acceptable sacrifice.

[handwritten margin notes: "Contrast", "example"]

What we see in this story has often been repeated in the life of the church. Thus, at some of the saddest times of the Middle Ages, ecclesiastical positions were bought and sold. If someone wished to become a bishop, he would buy the post and then seek to recover his investment by selling other positions that were now his to sell.

But it is not necessary to go that far back. Today, some have become millionaires by preaching on television. When, a few years ago, one of these "evangelists" was brought to public attention, it was found that even his doghouse was air-conditioned. Others have become rich by blessing and selling handkerchiefs, miraculous water, and books claiming to decipher the mystery of the ages.

What all this has in common with the merchants in the Temple is the use of religion to profit at the expense of the credulity of others. What do you think Jesus would say about religious practices today, especially those having to do with money?

Act: Look at your own checkbook or your tax returns and make a list of the causes you have supported with your donations. Have you taken care to make sure that they are really service organizations, and not programs for the benefit of those who promote them? Have you taken the time to learn how your local church and your denomination use their funds? Do you attend meetings where such decisions are made? When the next opportunity presents itself, remember that doing this is part of your own responsibility as a member of the church and as God's steward.

Second Day: Read John 3:1-8.

See: Today's passage is well known. An important Pharisee called Nicodemus comes to see Jesus. His name means "conqueror of the people." The reason for that name is not known. But we are told that he was a Pharisee and a "leader" of the synagogue. At this point it is important to remember that being a "Pharisee" did not mean that he was a hypocrite, which is what is often meant by that word in today's common usage. A Pharisee was simply a member of one of the main religious parties among Jews. The Pharisees were particularly well known because they sought to obey the Law in every detail and were constantly trying to discover how best to apply it in each situation. They were not evil or irreligious, but exactly the opposite. Jesus often criticizes them, not because they were evil, but rather because their religiosity and their very goodness could easily lapse into pride and legalism.

Nicodemus does not come to Jesus to question him, but rather to tell him that he and others know that Jesus has been sent by God. We are not told who those others were; but Nicodemus speaks in the plural: "we know."

Jesus' response does not seem to relate to what Nicodemus has just said. He simply tells his visitor that in order to enter the kingdom of God it is necessary to be born anew. Not surprisingly, Nicodemus is perplexed, and then Jesus compares the freedom of the Spirit with the freedom of the wind. The Greek word *pneuma* means both "Spirit" and "wind," as well as "breath."

Thus, these multiple meanings of a single word are used to relate the new birth and the new life with the Spirit of God, and in a way, also with birth and drawing breath. The wind is mysterious and free. No one knows where it comes from or where it goes, and it blows unexpectedly, whenever it wills. It is then that we feel and hear it. Likewise, the Spirit that gives breath to the new life is free, mysterious, and powerful.

Judge: In studying a passage as familiar as this one, we are tempted to take for granted that we already know what it says, and thus not to allow it to speak to us anew. Talk about being "born again" has become so common that sometimes we do not even listen. But when we stop to think about it, it is indeed something mysterious and astonishing. Nicodemus is right in asking, "How can anyone be born after having grown old? Can one enter a second time into the mother's womb and be born?" When we see him asking such questions, it is easy to think that he lacks understanding, whereas we know what Jesus is talking about. But Nicodemus at least knows that Jesus is talking about something radical and surprising, while we sometimes speak of the new birth as if it were as simple as changing shirts. But the truth is that this second birth is at least as astounding as the first birth—even more. This is why Jesus compares the Spirit with the wind: it is free to blow from wherever it wills, it cannot be guided by our wishes, and it may blow gently or fiercely, move a ship along or sink it. Likewise, the Spirit of God is both a gentle breeze and an overpowering presence.

This is a word that is both painful and joyful. It is painful because it implies that our present lives must be lost. It is joyful because it tells us that, no matter who we are or what we have done, by the power of the Spirit we may begin anew. Strange and impossible as it may seem, it *is* possible to erase the past; and bondage to the past is a most terrible servitude. What I did yesterday, or even years ago, limits what I can do today. So much of our energy goes into lamenting what we did or did not do! And indeed, we must lament and repent for many of our actions and decisions. But we seem to have little power to go beyond being sorry for our past. Oh, if things had simply been otherwise!

But Jesus tells Nicodemus—and us too—that things can be different. What we did or what we were does not have an ever-lasting grip on us. Thanks to this new birth brought about by the Spirit, we can face a new life, full of new possibilities. Our bondage to the past—to the sins of the past—is broken. This new life is a life of new freedom!

Act: Pray: "Dear God, who in your only begotten Son have promised us new life, take my life. Like a mighty wind, tear from it whatever is not pleasing to you. Create it anew, as you did in the beginning. Give me the joy and the hope of a new life. I pray in the name of Jesus, the Lord of all life and the Lord of my life. Amen."

Third Day: Read John 3:9-21.

See: The conversation between Jesus and Nicodemus continues. Nicodemus wants further explanations: "How can these things be?" This is not an unbelieving question, but rather one express-ing the desire to learn. He is intrigued by Jesus' words and wants to understand them.

Jesus responds at length, and his response includes some of the best-known verses in the Bible, such as John 3:16. It is impor-tant to note, however, that Jesus indicates that the new birth is the result of God's action, something that happens outside us, that we cannot achieve by ourselves; and yet, he says also that the possibility of this new birth is within our reach, that in a sense it does depend on us.

What does not depend on us, but is entirely God's initiative, is the gift of the only Son of God and his coming in order to be "raised"—on the cross and in his resurrection—as the serpent was raised by Moses in the desert. (The story is found in Numbers 21:9. Moses made a bronze serpent and put it on a pole. People who had been bitten by poisonous snakes could be saved by looking at this bronze serpent. To say that Jesus will be raised like this serpent means that by looking at him people will be saved and attain renewed life.)

On the other hand, what is left for humans to do is to believe.

The gift of the Son by itself is not enough. One must believe. God does not force anyone to be born again.

These two elements are interwoven in the well-known verse 16, where Jesus says that God "gave his only Son"—God's action—"so that everyone who believes"—the human response—"may not perish but may have eternal life"—the new life resulting from the new birth, a life in which God's action and ours are joined.

Note also that verse 17 stresses that all of this is a sign of God's love. Jesus did not come to condemn the world, but rather to save it. Even though rejecting salvation brings condemnation, the message is primarily one of salvation, of joy, of gift, of possibilities.

Judge: There is another side to the coin of new birth. It is not only the promise of new life. It is also the need to abandon the old. This is what Paul calls "dying in Christ." To wish to be born again and at the same time keep the old life is to lead a double life. If we insist on it, we forfeit the real joy and freedom of new life.

This means that the new birth is a very serious matter. Nicodemus, whom we often criticize for not understanding Jesus, understood at least that this new birth was something mysterious and overwhelming. Some Christians today take it so lightly that it appears to be a simple matter. That may be one of the reasons why so many Christians prefer not to even talk about the new birth. But that is no solution. What we must do is to take the new birth very seriously, and to be ready, not only to accept the new life that God offers, but also to leave behind the old life that God rejects.

To be born anew is not simply a matter of changing a few things that are obviously wrong in our lives, and then keep on with the rest as if nothing else had changed. To be born again is to begin anew. Paul speaks of this in the radical terms of an entirely new creation (2 Corinthians 5:17). He also declares that what he used to consider a gain he now regards as a loss (Philippians 3:7). To be born again is to put all things at God's disposal, so that God will do with them as God pleases—and this includes those things of which we are ashamed as well as those of which we are proud, that which we love as well as that which we hate.

The promise of new birth is true and dependable. There is no need to remain enslaved by our past. And the promise of new birth is also a challenge and a demand. It is impossible to take the one without the other.

Act: Repeat yesterday's prayer: "Dear God, who in your only begotten Son have promised us new life, take my life. Like a mighty wind, tear from it whatever is not pleasing to you. Create it anew, as you did in the beginning. Give me the joy and the hope of a new life. I pray in the name of Jesus, the Lord of all life and the Lord of my life. Amen."

Fourth Day: Read John 3:22-36.

See: Jesus has now begun his ministry, and John the Baptist continues his. In the passages we studied recently, Jesus was in Jerusalem and its surroundings. Now he is still in that area, in Judea, baptizing. John the Baptist is also baptizing, although "at Aenon near Salim." Exactly where this was is not known, although scholars tend to think that it was near the border between Galilee and Samaria. Thus, it would appear that John continues his ministry in the north, while Jesus is further south.

Someone comes to John and tells him that Jesus is also baptizing. It is not clear who these people are. They may be some of John's disciples, or they may be some of those who debated with John's followers (verse 25). What is apparent is that they are seeking to foster competition or mistrust between John and Jesus.

But John refuses to lend himself to such feelings. As he did before, he now declares once again that Jesus is the promised One, and is therefore greater than John himself. In order to explain this, John uses the image of a bridegroom and his friend: if the friend is a true friend, he rejoices in the bridegroom's joy. Likewise, John rejoices that Jesus has come. He then follows this declaration with a series of statements about Jesus' heavenly origin, his unique relationship with the Father, and so on.

Judge: We witness once again John the Baptist's firm but humble attitude. Last week we saw him refusing to hold center stage, and pointing toward Jesus. (Remember the example of a city and a sign pointing to it.) Here he once again refuses to compete with Jesus, as if it were a sort of popularity contest. On the contrary, John declares that he must decrease while Jesus increases.

Sometimes those of us who seek to follow Jesus and to bear witness to him find it very difficult to decrease. We wish to be acknowledged. We wish to be admired. We think we ought to be thanked. All of this is acceptable and even necessary up to a point, for every human being needs to be appreciated and acknowledged. But sometimes it goes so far that instead of pointing toward Jesus we stand in the way of others, as if what should be a billboard by the roadside had been placed in the middle of the road.

This is certainly a danger in the ministry of famous preachers and evangelists, who sometimes become so popular that people go to listen to them rather than to hear about Jesus. In response, true evangelists refuse to accept such excessive praise and tend to stand aside so that people may indeed see Jesus rather than them.

But every true believer runs the same risk. We seek to live in holiness, to help others, to study the Bible and to pray, to do God's will in every possible way. When we take such a path, there are many who acknowledge and admire us. This is not wrong. But when we receive such praise we must be very careful, lest we fall into the trap of competing with Jesus. We must constantly seek ways we may decrease, while Jesus increases.

Act: Have you sought to hide your own weakness and vulnerability, even in the community of the church? If so, could you be claiming for yourself a perfection you do not possess, and thereby undercutting your own witness to Jesus? Consider ways you

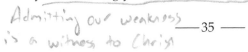

Admitting our weakness is a witness to Christ

can make it very clear that you depend on him, and are quite weak apart from the power that comes from him. Write down your reflections.

Fifth Day: Read John 4:1-42.

See: Today's passage is long, but quite familiar. It is the story of Jesus and the Samaritan woman at Jacob's well. Having learned of the Pharisees' attempt to drive a wedge between him and John the Baptist, Jesus decides to leave Judea and go to Galilee. This takes him into Samaria, where he meets the woman at the well.

Jesus is sitting by the well when a woman comes to draw water. Against all that was expected in that society—Jews did not speak to Samaritans, and male religious leaders did not converse freely with women—Jesus asks the woman for a drink of water. She expresses her surprise that Jesus talks to her. Jesus tells her that if she just knew who he is, she would ask *him* for water, and he would give her "living water." She thinks that he is referring to water in the literal sense and quite judiciously tells him that he has no bucket to draw water. Jesus tells her that this is a different sort of water, which quenches thirst forever.

At first she shows no more than the very practical interest in such miraculous water, which would save her the drudgery of coming to the well daily. Slowly, she realizes that Jesus is an unusual teacher, and then turns her attention to religious matters separating the Jews and the Samaritans. But Jesus will not allow the conversation to follow that path, and in the end tells her that he is the Christ, the long-expected Messiah.

The disciples, who had gone in search of food, now return, and are surprised at finding Jesus in this conversation with the Samaritan woman. She leaves her water jar and runs to the city to tell people of her wondrous conversation, wondering if indeed Jesus is the Messiah. The disciples offer him food, and when he tells them that he has a special kind of food, they are just as confused as was the woman when he first offered her water. Meanwhile, the woman is back in town, and those who hear her witness come to Jesus and invite him to stay with them—a Jew lodging with Samaritans—because they have believed in him thanks to the woman's testimony. Jesus remains in the city for two days, and the number of those who believe in him grows as they are able to hear him directly.

Judge: There are at least two important points to be made when thinking about this story. The first is that the life Jesus offers is an overflowing sort of life: "Those who drink of the water that I will give them will never be thirsty. The water that I will give will become in them a spring of water gushing up to eternal life."

Few images could express with equal strength the abundance of the life that Jesus offers. It is like a great thirst that has been quenched—quenched not momentarily, but forever. It is a thirst quenched in such a way that one can then bring relief to the thirst of others, like "a spring of water gushing up to eternal life."

We would probably find this image even more compelling if we lived in the very arid zones of the Middle East, where Jesus met this woman. For people living in those areas, thirst symbolizes a deep longing, a sense that something of the greatest importance is lacking. But physical thirst is never completely quenched; one has to drink again and again. The same is true of other longings. Those who long for moments of triumph are never satisfied, for each triumph simply raises the bar higher and higher. Thus, for many people life becomes a deep and unquenchable thirst: thirst for happiness, thirst for material goods, thirst for love, thirst for praise. And the more they receive of whatever it is they seek, the more they need of it.

The abundant life Jesus offers is very different. Abundant life finds its satisfaction in itself. Our longing for eternity, our longing for meaning, our longing for love—all of this is quenched in the living water that Jesus offers the Samaritan woman, and us too!

Second, this story shows Jesus overcoming the divisions established by human society. Jews and Samaritans would not speak to each other. Many men considered women to be inferior and even unclean. But Jesus surprises first the woman and then his disciples in breaking all such social and even religious conventions.

These two points are interrelated. The water that gushes forth for eternal life will acknowledge no human barrier. Whoever drinks of it will no longer be able to contain it within established and acceptable channels. The abundant life that Jesus offers is such that it spills over like running water, crossing every boundary and calling us to love those from whom we are separated by seemingly insurmountable obstacles, prejudices, and even hatreds.

It is clear that in our society—as in every human society—we like to classify people, and to set barriers between them: race, sex, class, age, and so forth. Quite often, those of us who feel excluded respond by building our own barriers and fences. But the water that gushes forth for life eternal, and the Lord who provides such water, will not allow us to do so.

Act: Think of someone from whom you are alienated by prejudice, by social practice, or even by some of your past history. Resolve to approach that person during the course of this coming week, and to offer some sign of the love of Christ. Write down your resolution, and leave room in your notebook so that later you can come back to this page and report the result and your reflections about it.

Sixth Day: Read John 4:43-54.

See: After spending two days in the Samaritan city, Jesus returns to Galilee. It was here that he had first shown his great power at the wedding in Cana. By now, some other Galileans who had been in Jerusalem at the time of Passover had returned telling of the wonders that Jesus had done in the capital city.

When Jesus was back in Cana, he received a visit from a "royal official"—that is, someone in Herod's service—whose son was ill in Capernaum. This man came to ask Jesus to heal his son. Instead of going with the official to Capernaum, as this man wanted, Jesus simply told him that his son was all right. The official believed him, and his faith was confirmed as he received news of his son's improvement. As a result, both he and his family believed.

John tells us that this was the "second sign" that Jesus did in Galilee—the first was at the wedding feast in Cana. In contrast with the other Gospels, which stress the ministry of Jesus in Galilee, John places much of his narrative in Judea and its capital, Jerusalem. As a result, this Gospel seems to deal more directly with the opposition of the Judeans to Jesus as a Galilean intruder.

Judge: Note that the royal official comes to faith, one might say, in stages. First he believes that Jesus can heal his son. Then he believes what Jesus tells him and leaves to return home. Finally, he believes when he learns that his son was healed just as Jesus told him.

Sometimes faith grows and develops in similar stages. One who already believes finds confirmation in other events, and such confirmation in turn produces deeper faith. Those who refuse to believe until they are confronted by an undeniable proof will most likely never come to faith.

This is a common experience among believers. Unbelievers often remain so because they are unwilling even to consider faith until they are forced into it. If in order to believe we need undeniable proof, then we are no longer dealing with belief. In truth, faith usually comes first, and its confirmation comes later.

Act: Pray: Lord, help me believe. I am not asking for proof. I am simply asking that you will increase and strengthen my faith. And I ask the same for others who today are studying this very story— that their faith too may increase. I pray in the name of Jesus, who did wonders in Galilee and still does them today. Amen.

Seventh Day: Read John 5:1-18.

See: Today's story takes place in Jerusalem. John tells us that there was a pool near one of the city gates whose waters had healing power. There were times when the water was stirred, and it was precisely then that one had to enter the water in order to be healed. Although we are not told how often this happened, apparently it was often enough for sick people to gather around the pool to wait for the appropriate time.

There was near the pool a man who had been ill for thirty-eight years, and who had now come to the pool hoping to be healed. But because of his infirmity he found it impossible to get to the pool when the water was stirred. His situation seemed hopeless until Jesus approached him, talked with him, and told him to take up his mat and walk—which he did!

However, this is not the end of the story, for the man who had been healed was approached by some extremely religious Judeans who asked who had dared heal him on the Sabbath. But the man could not answer, because Jesus had not identified himself and had simply left after the miracle. It was later, when Jesus met the man in the synagogue, that the man was able to tell who it was that had healed him. At this point, these religious leaders questioned Jesus, asking how it was that he had dared heal on the Sabbath. Jesus responds that just as his father, God, is working, so is he. This enrages his opponents even more, for he not only has broken the Sabbath, but has also claimed a special relationship to God.

The result of all of this is that these religious leaders of Judea begin to plot the death of Jesus, who seemed to ignore their religious principles by healing on the Sabbath, and who also seemed to blaspheme by claiming to be so close to God.

Judge: This story may lead our reflections in three directions, all of them important.

First, the story helps us understand something about how Jesus responds to human need. There are cases in which he waits for us to do all that is within our reach. There are others, such as the one in this story, in which there is hardly anything we can do. The man had no hope of being healed, since he could not reach the pool by himself, and he had no one to help him reach it. Sometimes we find ourselves in similar situations. From a purely human point of view, there is no way out. However, the God who made all things out of nothing can also do the impossible, and may tell us, like that man long ago, "rise, take up your mat, and walk."

Second, this text tells us much about how believers should seek to do good without expecting to be given credit for it. Jesus healed the man and simply left. The man did not even know who it was that had healed him. But we like to be given credit for our good deeds. If we perform a task for the church, we want our name to be mentioned, so that all will know that we were the ones who did it. If someone else is mentioned, and we are not, we feel offended and ignored. But Jesus acted very differently. He healed the man and then left. He did what he did because it was good, not because his good deed would be recognized.

Finally, the text reminds us that there is a sort of religiosity that is capable of doing more evil than good. Those who criticized the man because he was carrying his mat on the Sabbath were religious people. They did not do this because they were particularly evil people, or because they wished to oppose God's purposes. On the contrary, they were convinced that the law of the Sabbath was supreme—and let us not forget that the Sabbath had been commanded by God. Going around carrying a mat was to break the Sabbath. To heal someone on that day was equally seen as disobedience to the Law.

The rule they were defending was good. God had ordered a day of rest so that life could follow a rhythm of work and rest. But in their very efforts to obey that law as fully as possible, these ultrareligious people had twisted it. Instead of being a time of rest, the Sabbath had become a day of further difficulties and complications—a day on which one had to work hard at resting. Rest became an arduous obligation!

There are people whose religiosity is such that they insist on regulating everything, and who are therefore unable to see the action of God when it does not take place as they had determined it should. God performed a miracle. The man took up his mat and walked. Instead of glorifying God for this great deed, these people were concerned because all of this happened on the day of rest. They thought they were criticizing the man for carrying his mat, and Jesus for healing him; but in fact they were criticizing God for not resting when they had determined that even God should rest!

Do we ever act in a similar manner? Those of us who say we love God, are we ready to see God's action, and to glorify and praise God, even when this takes place in unexpected places?

Act: Make a list of the places where you have seen God's action recently. Make sure that your list does not include only events in church or things that have to do directly with religious matters, but also events in your community and in the world at large. Thank God for these signs of grace, wherever they may be. Share your list with others.

For Group Study

Invite the group as a whole to prepare a list like the one suggested above.

W E E K
THREE

First Day: Read John 5:19-29.

[handwritten: Main Point OT connection to X]

See: What we are studying today—as well as tomorrow—is the continuation of Jesus' response to those who sought to kill him—a speech that began in verse 17. At the beginning of today's passage, and also at the beginning of tomorrow's reading (verse 30), Jesus says that he does nothing on his own, but only what his Father wills. Those hearing him would understand that he was claiming God's authority for what he was doing, and this thanks to a special relationship that is based on love, for "the Father loves the Son and shows him all that he himself is doing." As a result of this love, the Father and the Son do the same deeds. The power and authority of the Son is such that the Father has left certain things up to him—in particular, judgment, for "the Father judges no one but has given all judgment to the Son."

Because of this intimate relationship, Jesus claims that those who believe in his word believe also in the One who has sent him. Furthermore, this word will be heard not only by Jesus' contemporaries, but the time will come when even the dead will hear and will be given the opportunity to believe and to live.

The passage ends with a reference to the final resurrection, when all shall rise at the summons of the Son—although some "to the resurrection of life," and others "to the resurrection of condemnation."

Judge: There are two important points in this passage. The first is that this passage clearly contradicts those who claim that God the Father is a God of justice, and that the Son is forgiving. Even

— 43 —

OT = very important

though such opinions are widespread in some churches, Jesus clearly declares that judgment is up to him—and this is not only for life, but also for condemnation.

The second point is that one of the reasons why the religious leadership of Judea opposes Jesus is that he claims to be on a par with God. Up to this point, they have only heard some passing words that would seem to indicate that Jesus is making such claims. But here Jesus declares that of which he is accused: he is on a par with the Father. He declares it quite openly, even though he must have known that this would only enhance enmity against him and eventually lead to his death.

This contrasts with the manner in which we often adjust what we have to say, in order not to displease our audience. If we know that a certain affirmation will not be well received, we remain silent, or we change the subject. Naturally, in this there is a measure of courtesy and consideration. We are not to go about saying things for the mere pleasure of offending others. But still, our speech and our attitudes must show integrity. When dealing with matters of serious significance, or in circumstances where remaining silent would lead others into significant error, we are called to speak the truth—even though this may result in losing friends or popularity.

Act: Resolve to speak "the truth in love" (Ephesians 4:15). This means avoiding giving offense to others, but at the same time telling the truth even when some might not like it. Write down this resolve. If you remember an occasion when you did not speak the truth in love, think about why you did it and what you could or should have said. Write down your reflections, as a future reminder.

Second Day: Read John 5:30-38.

Unity + b/w O

See: Jesus is still speaking to those who are upset by his teachings and actions, and who are plotting to kill him. Like the previous section, this one begins with his claim that "I can do nothing on my own." And, just as before, this does not mean that he is denying his own authority, but exactly the opposite, that he is claiming God's authority for himself. Whatever he does, he does because he seeks "to do not my own will but the will of him who sent me."

Jesus then turns to the subject of who it is that witnesses to him. First of all, he is not like charlatans who give testimony about themselves, praising themselves and declaring how good or how powerful they are. In verse 31 he says: "If I testify about myself, my testimony is not true." Although speaking in the first person—"if I"—Jesus is really stating a general principle: people who toot their own horn are not very believable.

The one who gives testimony on behalf of Jesus is "another" (verse 32). At first, Jesus does not state very clearly who this other is, for he sets out by referring to John the Baptist; but then he claims that his testimony comes from a much higher and worthy source. Even John's testimony is human, and the one giving testimony on behalf of Jesus is much greater than John the Baptist (verse 34). John was like "a burning and shining lamp"; but even so it is not on this testimony that Jesus bases his authority. The one witnessing on behalf of Jesus is none other than the Father!

The Father vouches for Jesus in two ways. The first, which is at the heart of today's Scripture, is by means of the works that Jesus does. "The works that the Father has given me to complete, the very works that I am doing, testify on my behalf that the Father has sent me" (verse 36). Thus, the very act of having healed the man by the pool—the work that has led to the accusations against him—is a sign that Jesus is truly sent by God. The second way in which the Father vouches for Jesus is through Scripture; but this we shall see in tomorrow's study.

Judge: This passage invites our reflection in two directions. First, it speaks of the unity between the Father and the Son, so that in seeing the Son we see the Father, and in Jesus we see God. This helps us understand the nature of God, and God's will for us. For instance, if Jesus heals on the Sabbath, the day of rest—which after all is the point under discussion in this entire episode—this means that God's love is such that it surpasses even God's Law. God wishes to have us worship and serve God; but this is because God knows that our true happiness is to be found in such worship and service.

Second, the passage invites our reflection on who it is that gives testimony on our behalf. The practice of witnessing for each other is quite common today, and not only in courts of justice—we speak of "references" or "letters of recommendation." When we apply for a job, we provide names of people who can testify on our behalf. Every time we use a credit card and the merchant calls the card's offices to have them authorize the purchase, someone is giving testimony about us—with the difference being that in this case the response the merchant receives is based on an entire series of testimonies that credit agencies have compiled over the years.

Given that we still use such practices, whose reference is most important for us? Letters of recommendation from former professors or employers? Credit reports? Is it not true that there is no more important reference than that of Jesus, who is to testify about us before the Father (see Matthew 10:32-33, and Revelation 3:5)?

Act: Imagine that you are writing a letter of reference, not about someone else, but about yourself, and that your letter is addressed to God. What would you say in your letter? Try it! In the end, you will find that you must commend yourself, not in your own name, but in the name of Jesus Christ, by whose merits we dare approach the Most High. Remember that the same is true of everyone else around you, no matter how holy or how sinful, how wise or how stupid, how powerful or how oppressed. We all have no other real commendation than the grace of Jesus Christ.

Third Day: Read John 5:39-47.

See: Jesus is still addressing those who have challenged him because he has dared heal on the Sabbath, and because he has put himself on a par with God. He insists that it is God who gives witness on his behalf; but he says also that the Scriptures witness to him. Since at that point the New Testament did not exist, he is obviously referring to the Hebrew Bible, or what we now call the Old Testament.

What Jesus tells these people is that they should study Scripture. They think they can find eternal life there; but in fact Scripture gives witness to Jesus, and it is he who gives eternal life. Thus, when his critics employ Scripture—in this case, the law regarding the Sabbath—to reject and condemn Jesus, they are in fact accusing themselves. They should realize that their enemy, the one who shows them to be wrong, is not Jesus, but Moses, whose Law points to Jesus. In short, by using Scripture to reject Jesus they are working for their own rejection.

Judge: What we have just read should tell us first of all that not everyone who quotes Scripture is necessarily right. Those religious leaders of Judea quoted Scripture in order to condemn Jesus for having healed on the Sabbath, and for having told the man to carry his mat on the Sabbath. If we look at the story of the temptation of Jesus in the desert, we will also see the devil quoting Scripture.

This means that there are ways of reading Scripture that are correct, and ways that are wrong. It is wrong to read Scripture as if it were a mere collection of laws. When we consult a lawyer with a problem, what the lawyer does is to consult the particular laws that might apply to our case. Other laws do not matter; indeed, it is as if they did not even exist. There are those who read the Bible in a similar fashion. They ask, for instance, "What does the Bible say about the Sabbath?" Or they ask about marriage or about the family or about what we should eat. They then find those verses that seem to refer to the question posed, and provide a final and inflexible answer. Whoever then does not obey what they declare to be the biblical laws on the matter is to be condemned and rejected. In response to such legalism, it is good to remember that all these things that the Bible says are important; but it is still wrong to place them at the center of our life and our faith, as if this were all that the Bible says.

The proper way to read Scripture, as we are shown in this passage, is to read it in such a way that Jesus stands at the center of our reading. In other words, the Bible, rather than a book of laws, is a book that tells us of the great and loving acts of God, and of God's blessings upon God's people—Israel and the church. At the very heart of the Bible stands the God who "so loved the world. . . ." It is a message of love, not of narrow legalism.

The point we must never forget is what Jesus says in verse 17: "My Father is still working, and I also am working." Legalists—be they Christian or Jewish—seem to forget that God is still active. They often seem to think that God gave us the Bible, and has left us alone with it. The Bible then becomes the legacy of an absent God. But Jesus tells us exactly the opposite. God is still working. Scripture tells us how God acted in the past; and this same God is still active. On the basis of our constant study of Scripture, we are to discern how God is acting today. The problem with those who challenged Jesus was that they were unable to see in the actions of Jesus the work of the same God who acted through Moses.

At what points are we inclined to read Scripture with a legalistic attitude similar to those who criticized Jesus? Could we, like them, be condemned by the very Bible we carry under our arms when we employ it to condemn others?

Act: Write in your notebook: "The central message of the Bible is God's action in Jesus Christ. The purpose of the Bible is to help us be part of that action. Whatever opposes it is not a proper reading of Scripture." Apply this principle to all your reading of Scripture throughout the rest of your "three months with John."

Feeding the SK

Fourth Day: Read John 6:1-15.

See: The narrative now moves to the western side of the Sea of Galilee, near the city of Tiberias—after which the lake was sometimes called the Sea of Tiberias. Jesus, however, is not in Tiberias, but elsewhere on the same shore of the lake.

The story is well known, since there are versions of it in every one of the four Gospels. John tells us that Jesus went with his disciples to a secluded place atop a mountain. But then he saw that a great multitude had learned that he was there and had come to him.

It is interesting to note that Jesus' first concern upon seeing the crowd was that they had no food. Later on in the narrative we shall see that there were important reasons why it was best for him to avoid such crowds. But for the time being, leaving such concerns aside, he sees to it that the hungry crowd has something to eat. He expresses that concern asking Philip how they will be able to buy bread for so many people. As elsewhere in his Gospel, John explains that the reason for such a question was not that Jesus did not know the answer, but rather to test Philip, who obviously has no answer. Two hundred *denarii* would not suffice—and this was a common laborer's salary for about ten months. Andrew, perhaps just in order to say something, mentions the loaves and fish that a boy has brought— even though it is clear that this will not even make a dent in the needs of the crowd.

It is then that Jesus takes charge of the situation. He orders that the people be made to recline on the ground, blesses the bit of food that he has on hand, and begins to distribute it among the disciples, who in turn distribute it to the crowd. The result is that everyone eats, and in the end there are twelve baskets of bread left over.

But there are other results John mentions, which we often do not see. The first is that the crowd is now convinced that Jesus is the awaited prophet, the Messiah. The second is that Jesus has to flee and hide for fear that the crowd will proclaim him king. Obviously, the two are interconnected.

Judge: Upon reflecting on this passage, and particularly on its ending, there are a number of learnings that may be drawn for the life of the church today. It is at the end of the story that we are told what was at stake when Jesus fed the crowd. He was running the risk that they would try to exalt him as king of the Jews, and that this would bring upon him the wrath, not only of the religious leaders who already were seeking to undo him, but also of the mighty Roman Empire. Remember that eventually Jesus would be crucified by the Romans, accused precisely of claiming to be king of the Jews. Therefore, having the crowd proclaim him king, even though he himself was making no such claim, would enhance his danger. Considering such likely consequences, Jesus could simply have sent the crowd away, and thus avoided conflict with the authorities or the need to hide. But that is not what Jesus does. He sees that they are hungry, and he feeds them.

Think now about how your church responds to the various needs in your community. Too often, when considering a need in our neighborhood, our first consideration is how a particular action on our part will affect the church and its standing in the community, rather than asking how a particular response meets the need. If, for instance, there are young people who spend their afternoons in idleness, with no other entertainment than getting into trouble, and someone suggests developing a program for these restless young people in the social hall of the church, we immediately worry about the possibility that our building will be damaged, or our insurance premiums will go up.

Does this sort of thing happen in your church or in others that you know? How can the church's service to the community be modeled after Jesus' response to the hungry crowd?

Act: Focus on a particular need in your community. Begin discussing it with other people in your church (or in several neighboring churches), in order to find ways to respond to that need. Write down your reflections, other people's responses, and how the project unfolds.

Fifth Day: Read John 6:16-21.

See: While Jesus is on the mountain, his disciples descend to the lakeshore, take a boat, and leave for Capernaum. It is evening, and John will later tell us that this was the only boat available. The Sea of Galilee is famous for its sudden storms, and in this case, one such storm catches the disciples at some distance from the shore—the Greek text says 25 or 30 *stadia*, which is about 4 or 5 miles.

They are in the middle of the storm when Jesus comes to them walking on the water. As one may well imagine, this causes them to be afraid. But Jesus identifies himself, and they welcome him into the boat. (This is the meaning of what the NRSV translates as "they wanted to take him into the boat.")

Judge: What I find surprising in this text, even beyond the miracle itself, is its simplicity. At other points in the Gospel of John, miracles are presented as "signs" of the power, authority, and mission of Jesus. But here it is simply Jesus' solution to a situation where he wishes to join his disciples, and no other boat is available. Jesus does not comment on the miracle, nor does he use it to teach something. He simply comes walking on water because that is the best way to join his disciples.

They in turn respond with similar simplicity. At first they are afraid, because they wonder who is this figure that they see approaching them over the surface of the water, through storm and darkness. But once Jesus identifies himself, they simply welcome him into the boat and continue on their journey.

This contrasts sharply with the way some Christians today boast about miracles and acts of healing. Some have television programs revolving around such miracles, and most of the time is devoted to people giving witness to having been healed. What we fail to see in such situations is that the very fact of making so much of a miracle, and being so astounded, is in itself the result of a lack of faith. It is as if one did not expect God to act, and is therefore completely surprised by God's action.

The faith of the disciples is more mature. They accept the miracle as one more action of the one whom they have seen performing other wonders. They know who their Lord is, and what he can do. Once they recognize Jesus, his walking on water is no longer something of which to be afraid or even surprised. What would be surprising would be for the Lord of such great power never to use it.

Act: Think about what God has done in your life. Remember extraordinary events and divine interventions; but remember also the ordinary. Make a list of places in your life where you saw—or where you now see—God acting. Consider in particular a problem or situation that for a while had you seriously worried, but now seems to have been left behind, or has lost its sting. End your period of study by writing down a prayer of thanksgiving for all the miracles that God has performed in your life.

Sixth Day: Read John 6:22-34.

See: At the dawn of next day, people seeking Jesus cannot find him. The previous afternoon they had seen the disciples leaving on the only boat that was available, and Jesus did not go with them. They obviously have no idea that Jesus has joined his disciples in the middle of the lake. At any rate, since other boats had now come in from Tiberias, they took those boats to Capernaum, where they expected to find Jesus' disciples, and thus to get a clue as to Jesus' whereabouts.

Upon arriving at Capernaum, they are surprised to find Jesus there. They ask him how he got there. But Jesus, rather than answering their question, tells them that they have followed him because he fed them, and not really because they believe in him. He then calls on them to work, not for the sort of food that perishes, but for the sort of food that remains in eternal life, which he is ready to give them. This is why they now ask how they can work for God. To this Jesus responds that the only work they must do is to believe in him. They claim that they would believe if Jesus gives them a "sign"—that is, a miracle. They add that Moses gave the people such signs by feeding them in the desert with manna. Jesus tells them that it was not Moses, but God, who gave their ancestors "bread from heaven," or manna, and that now the same God offers them "bread from heaven." They finally ask Jesus to give them this bread.

Judge: When you think about it, this is a surprising story. These are the same people whom Jesus fed the previous day through an apparently <u>unforgettable miracle,</u> and who now have followed him to Capernaum. Now, when Jesus tells them that they must believe in him, <u>they ask for a sign!</u> As if he had not given them one the day before! Yesterday, when they were hungry, they ate the bread and fish that Jesus provided. But today they are quite ready to forget that and ask for more miracles!

This is precisely the problem with faith that is based on miracles. If no more miracles are forthcoming, it wilts and even dies, like a plant that is not watered. <u>Such faith is quite common, and most of us are attracted by it.</u> Sometimes we even think that this is the highest form of faith. The result is a great number of believers who are always looking for a place where more wonders are evident, and thus go from evangelist to evangelist, from TV program to TV program, and from church to church, always seeking greater miracles, clearer "signs"—one could even say, more thrills in the faith.

Many of us know people who believed because they witnessed a wondrous event; and then, as the memory of that event faded, so did their faith, to the point that it became dormant, and they are no longer active believers. To a certain degree, many of us have also gone through such experiences. This is not a proper understanding of faith. Faith certainly holds to a God who can and does perform miracles; but it does not believe in God because God works miracles. Faith believes in God simply because it trusts God, loves God, seeks to serve God.

Act: Pray: Lord, I believe in you; help my unbelief. Give me faith. But give me the sort of faith that rejoices in your presence, that loves and serves you, no matter whether it sees wonders or not. Thanks for the wonders I have seen in my own life and in the lives of others. But I thank you above all for the wondrous miracle of your love, which is shown in so many ways, and particularly in Jesus Christ. In his name I pray. Amen.

Seventh Day: Read John 6:35-59.

See: Yesterday's text ended at the point where those who had come to Jesus asking for more miracles finally ask him for the "bread of heaven" that he had offered. Now the conversation continues, and Jesus explains to them what this "bread of heaven" is. In the end it is clear that he himself is the heavenly bread. In order to "feed" on him, one has to believe. Those who believe in him will have abundant life and will be raised on the final day. They will rise by the power of Jesus (verse 40).

It is here that John tells us that "the Jews" murmured against Jesus. As elsewhere in our study, we must be aware that in this context the phrase "the Jews" refers specifically to the Judeans, and particularly to their leadership—to those who, precisely because they were from Judea, considered themselves better Jews than the Galileans, and who therefore looked upon the latter with contempt and distrust. Thus, these who now murmur against Jesus are not necessarily, or even probably, the same people who first addressed Jesus and conversed with him. They are rather people who are listening to what Jesus says, but do not like it. What these people say is that they know Jesus, and even know his parents. Therefore, he cannot have come down from heaven. Jesus, knowing what they are thinking, tells them that if they fail to recognize him it is because they also ignore the Father, who bears witness to him.

The passage ends with a reiteration of what Jesus has already said. He is the heavenly bread, and this bread is even more life-giving and sustaining than manna from heaven. Those who ate of the manna eventually died; but those who eat of the heavenly bread that is Jesus will have eternal life (verse 54).

Judge: This passage uses an interesting metaphor for Jesus' saving work—a metaphor that we seldom employ. Jesus is depicted as our spiritual food. This image helps us gain a fuller picture of who Jesus is and how we are to relate to him. We often say that Jesus is our Savior, and that in order to share in that salvation we need to turn to him, cease trusting our own strength and resources, and put our trust in him. This is true; but it is also true that Jesus is our heavenly food. This means that the Christian life is a life lived in the constant company of Jesus, feeding on that company. We are fed by him as we walk with

Τρωγω vs ἐσθίω

eat   chew, gnaw, digest

him—as we shall see again when we study John 15:1-6. We live in Christ, not only because we had an experience of conversion, but also because our entire existence is nourished and sustained by Jesus, the bread of life.

Once again, do not forget that this entire conversation about feeding takes place immediately after, and as a result of, the feeding of the crowd. Jesus fed them even though he knew that this would not necessarily lead to them following him. He fed them simply because they were hungry and because he looks with compassion upon human need. Jesus offered them "bread from heaven" because that was precisely the reason for his being on earth. But he did not consider physical hunger unworthy of his attention. He did not feed the crowd so they would believe in him. He fed them simply because they were hungry.

We are to do likewise. If someone hungers after physical bread, we are to feed that person, no matter whether this will lead the person to faith or not. If someone hungers after the bread of heaven, we are to feed that person the bread of Jesus.

I have often witnessed discussions in which Christians argue about whether it is more important to feed the hungry than to preach to them, or about whether people should be fed when they come to the church only to get food or have another physical need met—the so-called rice Christians. Jesus' example leaves little room for such discussions. Physical bread is important. Spiritual bread is important. Hunger, in all its forms and manifestations, is against God's will. Therefore, as God's servants, we must feed those who hunger after physical bread as well as those who hunger after the bread from heaven.

Act: These Bible studies that you have undertaken on a regular basis are already a way you seek to be fed by the bread of heaven, which is none other than Jesus himself. Share this bread with others, perhaps by inviting them to follow the same program of studies, or perhaps by discussing with them some of the things you have learned or decided.

As you sit at the table for your next meal, resolve to share with those around you your concern over hunger in the world, and perhaps even in your community. Discuss with them how the mere fact that you have more than enough to eat places on you a responsibility to do something about the hunger of others.

For Group Study

At the end of the session, ask the group what they think we should do during the coming week to be fed by the bread of life, who is Jesus Christ. How can we help each other to be fed by that bread? Possibly some of the members of the group may wish to commit to pray for each other, or to gather at some other time during the week to discuss their spiritual life. Help them think, not only in terms of the group itself, but also of the wider congregation.

Ask the group to think also about what we can do to witness before our surrounding community that we do indeed believe in a Lord who is the bread of life, and who is concerned over human suffering and succors the needy. Are we actually presenting such a testimony? What can we do in order to improve and strengthen our testimony?

ybal health

W E E K
FOUR

First Day: Read John 6:60-71.

See: The words that Jesus spoke in the passage we studied yesterday proved offensive to many, including some of his disciples. The text does not explain why those words were offensive. Perhaps people were scandalized at the metaphor of eating his flesh and drinking his blood. (Remember that for a good Jew eating anything with blood in it was a breach of the Law.) Or perhaps people were scandalized because he dared compare his works with those of Moses, and to claim that he was above Moses. (Remember that in a text that we studied a few days ago Jesus had told his audience that those who ate of the manna in the desert still died, whereas those who would eat of the bread he had to give—himself—would live eternally.) Any good Jew would be offended by someone's claim to be even remotely comparable to Moses. Thus, there may have been more than one reason why Jesus' words seemed offensive to some.

Jesus does not back away. Nor does he soften his previous words. He simply insists on what he has said. Now he even claims that he will ascend to heaven (verse 62). And he claims that his words are more than any human reality (more than "flesh"), for they are "spirit and life."

On the other hand, he is not surprised at having many leave him, for according to John he already knew who believed and who did not (verse 64), and he even knew of the betrayal of Judas (verses 64 and 71). But he does use this opportunity to reinforce the commitment of his true followers. At the precise time when the crowds begin to turn away from him, Jesus asks the twelve: "Do you also wish to go away?" Peter responds with a radical confession of faith: "You have the words of eternal life. We have come to believe that you are the Holy One of God."

Judge: Peter's assertion becomes even more impressive precisely because it comes at the time when the crowds are turning away from Jesus. Jesus invites him to leave, and Peter responds by reaffirming his faith in Jesus.

It is easy to confess Jesus when all are supportive, and when that confession will not undercut our popularity. But confessing the faith is particularly significant when it is done in the midst of adverse circumstances, or in the face of contrary opinions.

At a certain point in his early career, famous missionary William Carey was facing enormous difficulties in India. He had run out of money. Another missionary had shamed the entire enterprise with his financial mismanagement. There was not even a single convert. So, he wrote to his friends in England, telling them his position was untenable, and that he had no option but to move forward. A person of less faith would have called for a retreat; but Carey forged ahead. This was what Peter did on this occasion. Is it what we do? Are you ready to confess your faith even in difficult circumstances? In your place of work or among your friends when people opt for actions that are clearly wrong, do you stand by your Christian convictions? If not, remember that the price is high, for as Peter said, only Jesus has the words of eternal life.

Act: Try to remember an occasion in which you were not faithful, perhaps because you feared the consequences, or perhaps by mere inertia. Try to remember another occasion when you were indeed faithful. Write down a brief summary of both. At the end of your study session, pray asking God to help you be faithful from now on, no matter how difficult the circumstances or how challenging the situation.

Second Day: Read John 7:1-9.

See: While reading this passage, it is important to remember that most often when John refers to "the Jews" he actually means those from Judea—best called "Judeans"—and particularly their leadership. This is why he now tells us that Jesus remained in Galilee "because the Jews were looking for an opportunity to kill him." In Judea, and particularly in Jerusalem, its capital, the religious leaders were plotting against Jesus. But in Galilee, which was also Jewish but was at some distance from Jerusalem, Jesus was safer.

The Festival of Booths was one of three great annual celebrations in Jerusalem. Small cabins or tabernacles were built—hence the name of "booths"—and it was customary for all male Jews to make an effort to attend the feast. Thus, it is not surprising that Jesus' brothers wished to go to Jerusalem, and that they suggested to Jesus that this would be a good opportunity to show his power.

Sadly, the reason that Jesus' brothers suggested this course of action was that they did not believe in him. They were taking no risk. If in Jerusalem Jesus turned out to be a false prophet, and was undone, this had nothing to do with them. If, on the other hand, he proved to be successful and was made a king, then they, his brothers, would certainly benefit from it.

Jesus tells them that his "time has not yet come." Remember that in the Gospel of John the "time" or the "hour" of Jesus is his death. Jesus is quite clear that the world will hate him. He will not be a popular hero. The world hates him because he speaks the truth about the world and its evil.

In the end, Jesus remains in Galilee while his brothers go to Jerusalem.

Judge: Consider the attitude of Jesus' brothers. They do not really believe in him. But just in case he does have real power, they urge him to go to Jerusalem and claim it. In short, they act neither out of faith nor out of love, but out of a sort of unbelief that can only believe in what is confirmed by power and triumph. If their brother actually turns out to be King of the Jews, they will rejoice. If not, they will feel sorry for him and go on with their own lives.

The same is true of many of us today. We are quite ready to

claim and to follow Christ as King. We wish to share in his triumphs. We want to be in the number of those rejoicing when he comes in glory. But we are not ready to share in the sufferings of the Crucified. We long for resurrection; but without a cross. We ask for forgiveness, but do not offer faithfulness.

The Christ of the Gospels is the Crucified King. We cannot claim his resurrection without claiming also his cross. We cannot enjoy the life he offers without dying with him. We cannot be raised with him if we are not also crucified with him. To claim otherwise is to partake in that same odd sort of unbelief that passes for faith that Jesus' brothers showed.

Act: Pray: "Lord, my God, teach me so to trust your Son that I may claim both his cross and his crown, both his victory and his sufferings. Crucify me with him, and with him bring me to life renewed. In difficult times, remind me of his resurrection. In times of ease, remind me of his cross. No matter what the times, let me live in him. Amen."

Third Day: Read John 7:10-24.

See: Although Jesus told his brothers he would not attend the feast, he eventually went. He went incognito; but apparently there was a rumor that he was in town, for his Judean enemies went looking for him. Note in verse 13 that the crowd, who are presumably all Jews, dare not speak openly "for fear of the Jews." This shows once again that in the Gospel of John the "Jews"—particularly those who oppose Jesus—are not all Jews in general, but the Judean leadership. At any rate, popular opinion is sharply divided, with some speaking favorably of Jesus and others claiming that he is a deceiver.

Finally, in the middle of the festival Jesus appears openly at the Temple and begins teaching. Now "the Jews" are astonished at his wisdom and learning, which he has apparently attained without schooling. Although we are not told that they posed this question directly to Jesus, he answered them by declaring that his teaching was not his, "but his who sent me"—that is, the Father's. Anyone who truly seeks to serve God will recognize what Jesus teaches as the truth and not his own invention. Those who speak on their own account, Jesus says, seek their own glory, while the one who seeks the glory of the one who sent him—that is, Jesus, sent by the Father—is true.

Jesus now refers to those who are seeking to kill him (remember John 5:18), telling them that they have the Law of Moses, but will not obey it. Note that Jesus does not say that the Law is evil. The problem is that these religious leaders who themselves do not obey the Law are seeking to kill Jesus because he healed someone on the Sabbath. This implies that these people have other reasons for enmity against him, and thus he asks: "Why are you looking for an opportunity to kill me?" The crowd, who are not aware of the plans that the powerful are making to rid themselves of Jesus, think that he is mad, possessed by a demon.

Once again, Jesus shows the absurdity of the accusations against him. The Judean leaders themselves circumcise on the Sabbath as well as on any other day. They do this because both the Sabbath and circumcision are part of the Law of Moses. Loving one's neighbor is part of the Law too. Why then condemn Jesus, who has obeyed God's will of love by healing the sick, even though he did so on the Sabbath?

The passage ends with a final exhortation from Jesus (verse 24), inviting his hearers to "judge with right judgment" and not be carried away by customs or appearances.

Judge: It is not always easy to "judge with right judgment." Quite often, in real life, one principle conflicts with another. Jesus shows this contradiction by using the example of circumcision. The Law commands that every male child is to be circumcised on the eighth day. The Law also commands resting on the Sabbath. It had already been determined that when these two principles clashed, a child should be circumcised on the eighth day, even if this happened to be the Sabbath. What Jesus had done was to heal a man on the Sabbath. The Law clearly commanded persons to take care of the sick and the infirm. But now "the Jews"—that is, the religious leadership—insist that Jesus has disobeyed the Law.

When seen in that light, it is clear that these Judean leaders judge matters in different ways according to their convenience. While it is acceptable to circumcise on the Sabbath—which they do—it is not acceptable to heal on the Sabbath—which Jesus did. The inevitable conclusion is that they are actually speaking on their own account and seeking their own glory. In these cases where principles conflict with each other, it is very important for us to seek to judge, not on our own account and for our own glory, comfort or convenience; but for the glory and the will of God.

Consider again the matter of using church facilities for housing the homeless. Obviously, we have an obligation to take care of buildings that have been entrusted to us—or that we have built—for the service of God. To provide shelter for the homeless is also good, and there is ample biblical support for it. But there seems to be a conflict between these two, for it is quite likely that using the facilities for providing shelter for the homeless will damage the facilities themselves. Thus, there will likely be a debate within the congregation as to what should be done and how. When the congregation or its leaders gather to decide what is to be done, if each side insists that it is right—if they insist on their own glory—they will never come to an agreement. If, on the other hand, they all seek the glory of God and are willing to modify their positions for that glory, it is more likely that they will come to a solution.

Act: Mentally review a disagreement or debate you have recently had with someone. In that disagreement, <u>were you really trying to find the best way to go, or were you simply trying to show that you were right and the other person was wrong?</u>

Next time you find yourself in disagreement with another, resolve to seek the truth and the glory of God, rather than simply trying to show that you know best.

Fourth Day: Read John 7:25-31. *Political naiveté*

See: Seeing Jesus teaching openly at the Temple, some among the crowd come to the conclusion that perhaps he has been able to convince the religious authorities that he is indeed the

Messiah. But they still wonder how this can be, since they know that Jesus has come from Galilee, and they expect the Messiah to come suddenly and mysteriously.

Knowing what they are saying, Jesus corrects them. He tells them that they do know where he has come from—Galilee—but the important question is not where he has arrived from, but who has sent him. The one who has sent him is true. Given the circumlocutions of pious Jews at the time, to speak of "the true" was a way of referring to God. Thus, what Jesus is saying is that, although he has arrived from Galilee, he has been sent by God.

There is then a disagreement among his listeners. Some seek to arrest him. Since only the religious leadership had the authority to do so in the Temple, one may well surmise that these are the sort of people whom John calls "the Jews," that is, the religious elite of Judea. But there are also among the crowd many who do believe that Jesus is the Messiah—the Christ, or Anointed One. For this reason, his enemies do not dare arrest him. And then John offers us a theological explanation for this: because his time had not yet come.

Judge: Upon reading this narrative, we may find people's credulity surprising. They think that perhaps Jesus has convinced the authorities that he is the Messiah. This shows their political naïveté, for they should have understood that the coming of the Messiah would pose serious difficulties for those religious leaders. Their authority is grounded on their religious expertise and their functions in the Temple, and quite likely most of them are sincere believers and faithful Jews. But their authority also comes from the Roman Empire, which has decided to allow the practice of the Jewish religion as long as it does not challenge Roman power, and which has also had a hand in appointing some of the higher echelons of the priesthood. People such as Herod and the High Priest held such offices thanks to Rome. Thus, the coming of the Messiah and the restoration of David's throne would put an end to much of the power of the present Judean elite. This is the main reason they oppose Jesus. But those in the crowd who think that Jesus has permission to preach because he has convinced the leadership that he is the Messiah do not seem to take this into account.

Actually, opposition to Jesus had two facets, one of them religious and the other political. The religious leadership was offended by seeing Jesus heal on the Sabbath, and then by his polemic with them precisely on this point. The political leadership was well aware that if the rumor spread that Jesus was the expected King of the Jews, Rome would intervene, would probably take away the measure of freedom that Judea has been granted, and would certainly blame the present leadership for not having handled the situation more adroitly.

As believers, we must take care lest we succumb to similar political naïveté. We are constantly faced with political leaders who seek the support of the church—or at least of Christians as such. Some of them are quite ready to say whatever they think Christians like to hear. Through the centuries, and to this day, there have been political leaders who have attained power with Christian support, and who then use that power to enrich themselves and their cronies at the expense of the working poor. Their words are inspiring, and some quote the Bible repeatedly. They use their words, their visits to churches, and the media to convince sincere but naive believers that they seek to do God's will, when in fact what they seek is power.

Act: Take a careful look at every political party or candidate that claims they are following Christian principles or inspiration. Do not let yourself be swayed by beautiful words or by quotes from the Bible. Do not let yourself be swayed even by their profession of faith, or by their taking up the banner of an issue of concern for Christians. Remember that in the Bible we are repeatedly urged to be particularly concerned for those who have little or no protection: widows, the poor, orphans, and foreigners. As you think of your civic and political participation, use this as a measuring rod for every politician, every law, and every action.

Fifth Day: Read John 7:32-39.

See: The religious leadership—the Pharisees and chief priests—upon learning what is being said about Jesus, decide that the time has come to have him arrested, and order that this be done. Later on we shall see the outcome of this command. Today we shall study Jesus' response when he learns that he is to be arrested, and how people react to his response.

Jesus tells them that he will not always be with them. It is not clear whether he says this only to his disciples, or also to those who are charged with the task of arresting him. At any rate, John does tell us that those who heard Jesus were more than the small circle of his closest disciples (7:35-40). Those who hear wonder what Jesus might mean by saying that he is going where he cannot be found. In the context of the existing circumstances, with the Temple police ready to arrest him, Jesus seems to be saying that he has a secret hiding place where he can flee and not be arrested. This is why some think that he is talking about fleeing "to the Dispersion among the Greeks" (7:35). This is a reference to the millions of Jews who lived beyond the borders of Judea and the Holy Land, in the Hellenistic world. Thus, they suspect that Jesus is about to go into exile.

Judge: When Jesus says that he is going to a place where he cannot be found, his listeners can only imagine that he is planning to leave the country and go to live among the Jews of the Dispersion—or that he is planning to hide in some secret place. Their frame of reference does not include other alternatives. However, Jesus is not speaking simply about going somewhere else on earth, but of a much more radical alternative. There is another option that his hearers cannot even suspect.

Today there are many of us, and also many movements claiming our allegiance, that can only think in bipolar alternatives— that is, of alternatives that exist only in pairs, so that if we reject one we fall automatically into the other. If you are not a Republican, you must be a Democrat. If you are not a Democrat, you must be a Republican. If you criticize capitalism, you must be a communist. If you do not like communism, you must favor capitalism. If you are not a fundamentalist, you are a modernist. If you are not a modernist, you must be a fundamentalist. When we allow ourselves to be trapped within such polarities, quite often we miss the most creative and promising alternatives. Sometimes there are options that completely leave aside both bipolar alternatives; and sometimes there are options that take something good from each of them. Thus, even within the context of our daily living and our societal arrangements, it is best not to allow ourselves to be limited by bipolar choices.

This is even more important when dealing with our faith. Most often, bipolar choices, precisely by claiming that there are no other options, leave God aside—for God does not really belong to any side. Those who heard Jesus thought that if he left Judea he must go to the Dispersion. In so doing, they discounted a third and higher possibility: that Jesus would go to be with God. Likewise, when today we think that there are only two opposite choices, and that these are given and fixed, we do not allow God to give us new answers.

Act: Next time you find yourself in a discussion or debate, stop to pray in silence. Ask God to show you better solutions than those being offered. You may be surprised!

Sixth Day: Read John 7:40-52.

See: Jesus' words cause division among the crowd. Upon hearing him, some would be convinced that he was the Messiah. But others felt that this could not be the case because he was a Galilean. Some claimed that the Messiah would come from Bethlehem in Judea. Others insisted that he could not come from Galilee, a region considered inferior by Judeans. In the midst of that disagreement, those who wanted to arrest him did not.

Thus, the Temple police return to the Pharisees and the chief priests who had sent them to arrest Jesus, but they do so empty-handed. When they are asked for a report, they simply say, "Never has anyone spoken like this!"

The response of the Pharisees is typical. They accuse the Temple police of allowing themselves to be convinced by Jesus. Then they claim that no one who is anybody—that is, the rulers and the Pharisees themselves—has believed in him. It is only those in the crowd, ignorant people who do not know the Law, who are swayed by Jesus, and they are therefore accursed.

At this point Nicodemus, who earlier had come to Jesus at night (John 3), speaks out. He does not defend Jesus openly, but simply asks that the legal process be followed and that Jesus not be condemned before being given a fair hearing. But, even though Nicodemus himself is a Pharisee and "a leader of the Jews" (3:1), as soon as he seems to defend Jesus the rest turn against him: "Surely you are not also from Galilee are you?" Then they justify their attitude with apparent biblical authority: "Search and you will see that no prophet is to arise from Galilee" (7:52).

Judge: The prejudice of Judeans against Galileans is clearly seen here. Note that it is not even all Judeans, but only some of the important people and the Pharisees who show this prejudice. These people look down on Galileans and any others who do not know the Law as well as they do. They even seem to think that any who are not at their level of knowledge are accursed, and when Nicodemus speaks out he is immediately classified as "a Galilean" in order to silence him.

Thus, what is taking place here is not a purely religious conflict. It is also a social and cultural conflict. The leaders of Judea think ill of all Galileans, who from their perspective are almost heathen. Now that these Galileans have appeared in Jerusalem and are claiming for themselves the promised Messiah, these Judean leaders see their ancient privileges threatened.

Something similar happens in our day, not only in religion, but also in matters political and social. Quite often, recent immigrants and other minorities are marginalized precisely because those who have traditionally held positions of privilege feel threatened. The same also happens in the life of the church. Practically every major denomination in the United States is discussing how to attract more Hispanics and other minorities; but none of those denominations is ready to allow these prospective newcomers to change or to challenge the ways things have traditionally been done. Let them join indeed, but let them join only on our own terms. It is often said that it is important to defend the traditional values and procedures of the denomination. But in fact, there is also fear that the newcomers will erode the power and prestige of the dominant group. Something similar happens in local congregations as well.

Act: Find out what minority groups are most numerous in your neighborhood. What is your church doing to make them welcome? Try to learn if your denomination has resources available to you and your congregation to help you take the message to these people and bring them into your church as fully participating brothers and sisters.

Seventh Day: Read John 8:1-11.

See: In past days we have seen various people come to Jesus: Andrew, Simon, Nathaniel, Nicodemus, and the Temple police. These people come for various reasons—some to question Jesus, some to follow him, and some even to arrest him—but all come voluntarily.

Today's story is different in this respect, for the woman did not come voluntarily to Jesus, but was forcefully brought to him. It is a woman caught in adultery that a group of scribes and Pharisees bring to Jesus in order to challenge him to deal with the case according to the Law, which demanded that such a woman be stoned to death.

There are, however, two important points that we often miss. The first is that the Law (Leviticus 20:10) established that in the case of adultery both the man and the woman should be put to death. If the woman was caught in the act itself, she certainly was not alone! Why then do these Pharisees and scribes bring only the woman and not the man? Perhaps because in that society, as in ours, it was thought that sexual sins on the part of a woman were more serious than the same sins on the part of a man. Or perhaps it was because, as we shall see, these people were less interested in the woman herself than in putting Jesus in a difficult position.

The second point we must remember is that the land was under Roman rule, and the Jews did not have the right to impose a death penalty. Therefore, these scribes and Pharisees are trying to place Jesus in an untenable position. If he says that the woman is to be killed, he will have to face Roman authorities. If he says that the Law of Moses is not to be obeyed, he will lose his credibility among the people. This is why verse 6 says that they did this "to test him."

For these scribes and Pharisees, the woman is simply a convenient instrument, an excuse to test Jesus. The fact that she has been discovered in a tragic situation—all the pain that may be behind her actions—and even the possibility that she may be stoned to death do not seem to matter. What is important is to test Jesus, to see whether he will support the Law of Moses or the law of Rome. If the woman is a sinner, these scribes and Pharisees are even greater sinners, for they are willing to crush her to reach their goals—and in this case their sin is compounded because they try to hide their petty motives behind a facade of religion.

Jesus responds by showing them their sin. What he wrote on the ground is not known. Some have thought that he was writing a list of possible sins. Others suggest that he wrote the Law from Leviticus, so that the accusers would realize that they were applying it unjustly. Still others think that he was simply doo- *Not* dling while people reflected on his words. Whatever the case *likely* may be, when Jesus told them that in order to cast the first stone one should be without sin, no one dared make such a claim, "and they went away one by one." Jesus then forgave the woman and told her to sin no more.

Judge: The most outstanding trait of the entire passage is the mercy of Jesus, which is available to all of us. Jesus did not tell the woman that what she did was right; but he did forgive her and told her to sin no more. The Jesus who forgave that woman forgives each one of us as we come to him asking for pardon.

On the other hand, in reading this passage we should not put ourselves only in the place of the woman whom Jesus forgave. We must also ask ourselves if there are cases in which our attitudes or our acts have been like those of the scribes and Pharisees. The church must certainly decry all that is against

God's will. But in so doing, we must take care lest our attitudes and our actions deny the love and forgiveness that are also part of God's will.

Too often religion is used, not to proclaim God's pardon and invite people to do God's will, but rather to show others that we are better than they. Then we begin to apply to them all sorts of rules to make it clear that they are dreadful sinners. And such rules are not always applied evenly, as we can see in the case of those scribes and Pharisees who let the man go and brought the woman to Jesus. Therefore, it is important to remember that in this passage Jesus confronted not only the woman, but also the scribes and Pharisees. Their sin—and also often ours—was at least as serious as the sin of the accused woman. Remember also that, precisely because she came knowing she was a sinner and they came believing they were good and pure folk, she received forgiveness and they simply drifted away.

Act: Think about someone in your church or in your community whom for any reason you consider a serious sinner. Now write in your notebook: "I need God's forgiveness just as much as _____."

Take some time to think about the reasons why what you wrote is true. Write down your reflections. Pray, asking forgiveness both for yourself and for that other person.

For Group Study

Write the following paragraph on the blackboard or on newsprint:

> The message of the church is not only that God hates evil and that this evil includes immorality, vice, and exploitation. The message of the church is also that those who commit these sins may be forgiven by the God who says "Go and sin no more."

Discuss this paragraph with the group. Ask them if, in our daily lives and in our congregational practices, we give witness more frequently to the first of these statements than to the second.

W E E K
FIVE

First Day: Read John 8:12-20.

See: The text tells us that Jesus "spoke to them," but does not tell us exactly who his audience was. Since at the end we are told that Jesus spoke these words "while he was teaching in the treasury of the temple," one may surmise that Jesus was probably speaking to any who would listen.

Jesus often spoke about himself, particularly in the Gospel of John. What in others would have been egocentric or undue self-admiration makes sense in the case of Jesus, whom John presents as Lord and Savior, and who therefore must invite others to believe in him. This is why the phrase "I am" appears so often in the Gospels, and particularly in John. Earlier, in John 6:35, we saw him declaring, "I am the bread of life." Now he says, "I am the light of the world," adding that those who follow him "will have the light of life."

It is not surprising that the Pharisees would challenge such claims. In today's passage, the challenge is on the issue of who it is whose witness certifies Jesus' authority. The Pharisees tell Jesus that, since it is he who certifies himself, such certification is not valid. In Spanish, we have a phrase to comment on those who commend themselves, of whom we say "the recommendation comes from someone who is too close to him."

Jesus responds that, even though he testifies for himself, what he says is true. Then follows a series of claims that eventually his disciples would come to understand, but that the Pharisees can neither understand nor accept. Believers will understand that Jesus is referring to his origin with the Father, and to his

— 71 —

close relationship with the Father. But the Pharisees take his words literally; just as earlier they understood his words to mean that he would go elsewhere. It is for this reason that they ask: "Where is your Father?" Jesus' answer—once again cryptic for the Pharisees, but quite clear for those who believe in him— is that he is so close to the Father that those who know him also know the Father. The clear implication is that the Pharisees do not know the Father.

Judge: What Jesus says is that those who know him know the Father. This is a fundamental tenet of the Christian faith, which affirms that in Jesus we see God. The best way to come to know God is not by philosophical speculation, or—as some claim today—by means of silent meditation. The best way to come to know God is by studying the life and teachings of Jesus, and by so following him that he comes to live in us.

Agree?

Starting from that experience, we can see God more clearly, not only in Jesus, but also in nature, in the beauty of the arts, in human love, and in the harmonious movement of the heavenly bodies. But all of this builds on the experience of Jesus Christ— without which we risk inventing a false God, one who is in fact an idol.

Act: We are now about a third of the way through our study of the Gospel of John. Review what you have learned, thought, and done during this time. Are you coming to know Jesus better? Are you now any closer to him? Are you more devoted to his service? Are you finding better ways to serve others and to show God's love for them? Pray that your heart may be filled by him, and that through him, you may come to know the Father.

Has this helped?

Second Day: Read John 8:21-30.

See: Jesus' words are still rather cryptic, except for those who believe in him. He announces that he is leaving and that those who are now listening to him will search for him, but will not find him. From the earliest times, Christians have understood these words of Jesus as an announcement of his death, resurrection, and ascension. He will leave, and those who will look for him in the tomb will not find him. In the story itself, those who first heard these words and did not believe in him misunderstood what he was saying. They take it literally, and some even think that he may be contemplating suicide. But Jesus simply tells them that they cannot understand: "You are from below, I am from above; you are of this world, I am not of this world." This does not mean simply that he has come from heaven, but also that their perspective is not heaven's perspective. Their perspective is of this world, and this is why they neither see nor understand. And because they do not see and do not understand, they will die in their sins. Still some do not believe, and he simply says that they will not understand until they "have lifted up the Son of Man"—that is, when they have crucified him.

What is probably most surprising about this entire passage is that, even though Jesus seems to be speaking in riddles, John tells us that "as he was saying these things, many believed in him."

Judge: There is a complex relationship between understanding and believing. Sometimes we imagine that if we truly understood God's designs, we would certainly believe. Or we think the opposite—believing is enough, and understanding is not important. But the truth is that believing and understanding go hand in hand, so that each of the two strengthens and supports the other. In this case, the Pharisees and other experts on the Law do not understand what Jesus says. In contrast, others believe, and therefore come to understand what Jesus is saying—at least in part.

The same is true today. If we decide that we must wait until we understand every point of Christian doctrine, and have solved every mystery and every intellectual difficulty, we shall never believe. On the other hand, if we say that faith is enough and it is not necessary to understand the things of God, we shall never understand, and in the end faith itself will be weakened. Christian discipleship joins the two. The more we believe, the better we understand; and the more we understand, the better we believe.

Act: Pray: "My God, your wisdom is great. It is high, and I cannot understand it. But I pray that, through faith, you will give me the wisdom to understand more and to serve you better. In the name of Jesus, your wisdom and your revelation. Amen."

Third Day: Read John 8:31-41a.

See: The words are familiar: "You will know the truth, and the truth will make you free." But we seldom think of the context in which they appear. This passage is a conversation between Jesus and a group of Judeans who had believed in him; but in the end (8:59) they will try to stone him to death.

How could it be that these people who had believed in Jesus turned so violently against him? As we read the entire story we come to the realization that the core of their disgust is precisely in the words, "you will know the truth, and the truth will make you free." This is a hint that these words have a cutting edge we do not usually suspect, for those who first heard them were offended.

The story tells us that these believers were offended upon hearing Jesus promise them freedom. They claimed they had never been slaves, so for Jesus to promise them freedom is offensive and tantamount to calling them slaves. Jesus tells them that, as sinners, they are indeed slaves of sin, and need the liberation he has to offer. He further adds that, although they are children of Abraham, they do not follow Abraham but another.

Judge: It is interesting to note that these Judeans, who claim that they are children of Abraham, also claim that they have never been enslaved. They seem to forget that the entire people of Israel was enslaved in Egypt, that centuries later they were taken as captives to Babylon, that at various times they had been subjected to the Philistines, to the Amorites, and to many others. They also are forgetting that they now live in an occupied province under strict Roman rule. And it is precisely because they have forgotten these things—or rather, because they would like to forget them—that they are unwilling to hear the freeing word of Jesus.

What does all of this have to tell us? It certainly means that if we deny our own need and misery we shall also be rejecting the freedom that Jesus offers. Those who are healthy have no need of medication. Those who are free do not need to be liberated— they cannot be liberated. If Jesus is physician and liberator but we are neither sick nor enslaved, we cannot use much of what he can do for us.

We live in a society where it is difficult to admit that we have problems, for such an admission is seen as a sign of failure or of weakness. This even pervades the life of the church, where there are often people who are deeply concerned, for instance, because they are unemployed and cannot pay their mortgage, but do not dare express their concerns and their sufferings to their brothers and sisters. There are many who seem to think that in order to be part of the fellowship of the church they must conceal their weaknesses, their sins, and their doubts. Even worse, quite often it is the church itself that promotes such notions.

Just as those Judeans could not be truly free until they acknowledged their enslavement, we cannot be truly healed until we admit our disease, nor can we be truly free until we confess our own enslavement. The truth that will set us free must begin by admitting who we truly are and what our needs truly are. Confessing that truth is the first step in confronting the "father of lies" (8:44) and receiving the Lord of all truth, the only one who can make us truly free.

Those Judeans were living out of the lie that they were free, and that lie kept them from the truth that could have made them truly free. What are the lies in which we live today, and which keep us from the Father of all truth?

Act: Pray: "My God and Father of my Lord Jesus Christ, I thank you for your liberating truth. I thank you that I have found that truth in Jesus Christ. I pray that you will help me be rid of all falsehood standing between my life and the freedom that Jesus offers. In his name I ask this. Amen."

Fourth Day: Read John 8:41b-47.

See: The conversation continues. It turns increasingly acrimonious and even violent, for these Judeans insist that they are children of Abraham, and Jesus persists in telling them otherwise. They are offended, for Jesus is practically declaring them to be illegitimate children (8:41). But Jesus holds his course. He declares that his interlocutors are children, not of Abraham, but of the devil, and what they seek to do is to fulfill the devil's designs.

The passage ends with a brief speech in which Jesus marks the contrast between the children of the devil and the children of God. The devil is "the father of all lies"—which implies that these people whom Jesus declares to be children of the devil are themselves liars. It is because they are children of the father of lies that these people—who formerly had believed in him—reject what Jesus says. If they belonged to God, they would listen to the words from God and would believe in Jesus, whom God has sent.

Judge: We have already noted that there is a strong connection between believing and understanding. Today we note a similar relationship between doing and believing, between obedience and faith. These Judeans do not believe because they do not wish to obey; and they do not obey because they do not believe.

It is important to note that we run the risk of doing likewise. Some say that, if they had undeniable proof, they would believe and would also obey. But the truth is that the main reason why we doubt is that we do not wish to obey. In that case, lack of belief becomes a convenient excuse for disobedience. Here is an example. Someone told me recently that if he really had faith, he would leave his present career and begin preparing for the ordained ministry. He has received a call; but does not really wish to obey, for he knows that the price would be high. He then excuses himself by saying—and convincing himself—that he needs further proof. Were he to take the risk and begin the journey, proof would be given to him along the way.

In the case of these Judeans who had believed in Jesus, their disobedience was such that in the end they disbelieved, and Jesus declared them to be children of the devil, or of the "father of lies." Let us who have believed in Jesus take care, lest our lack of obedience be such that in the end we abandon him and become servants of "the father of lies."

Act: Pray: Lord, I wish to obey you right now, and for the rest of my days. Help me be faithful. Give me, not only faith, but also obedience; and not only obedience, but also faith. Take my steps and lead me along the way. In the name of Jesus, your Son, and the only true Way. Amen.

Fifth Day: Read John 8:48-59.

See: The dialogue goes on. Remember, these were people who had believed in Jesus. Now they are so disgusted with what he says that they try to insult him by calling him a Samaritan and saying that he has a demon. It is interesting to note that Jesus does not respond to the epithet of "Samaritan." After all, the Samaritans are simply another people, and therefore to call Jesus by this name is not the insult that the Judeans wish it to be. As to having a demon, Jesus denies it categorically, declaring that what is actually happening is that he honors the Father, and for that reason the children of the father of lies cannot honor him.

Jesus adds that those who keep his word will never die. This is further reason for scandalizing his interlocutors, who point out to him that even Abraham died, and that therefore Jesus is claiming to be greater than Abraham.

Here we are back to the cosmic perspective in which the Gospel of John presents the life and teachings of Jesus. Just as in John 1:1 we are told that the Word was in the beginning, here we are told that Jesus existed long before Abraham. The result of such a claim is that these former believers now take up stones in order to kill Jesus, because they take his words to be blasphemy. But somehow Jesus evades them and leaves the Temple.

Judge: A detail in this story that we often miss is that when his critics intend to offend Jesus by calling him a "Samaritan," he does not even acknowledge the intended insult. This indicates that Jesus does not find the epithet offensive. It may be so for these Judeans who think they are better than any Samaritan; but Jesus knows that such is not the case. His attitude here is similar to that other occasion when he took a Samaritan as an example in order to shame the religious leaders of Judea (Luke 10:30-36).

In our society it is quite common to use racist or sexist epithets to insult others. Taking such epithets as insults sometimes implies that being a member of the alluded group is indeed being inferior, and thus our negative reaction to such an epithet is in fact an affirmation of racism or chauvinism. In other cases, what people seek to do by developing and using racist epithets is to try to define the reality of those who are different from themselves. But those who called Jesus a "Samaritan" were in fact insulting themselves much more than Jesus. They deserve not anger, but rather pity. The best reaction is not a counter-insult, but a response of such dignity and integrity that it becomes clear that the intended insult cannot even touch us.

Act: Discuss with a group in your church or community how racism, sexism, nationalism, and all sorts of prejudice are manifest in our society. Make an inventory of your own conversations and actions during the last week, to see if you have fallen prey to some of these prejudices. Write your reflections.

Sixth Day: Read John 9:1-12.

See: Today's narrative is similar to what we studied some days ago about the healing of a man on the Sabbath. Tomorrow, after having read the entire chapter, we shall see that once again the problem seems to be that Jesus healed someone—in this case a blind man—on the Sabbath. I say "seems to be," because the truth is that the religious leaders resent Jesus' actions and authority, and the only objection they can raise with some semblance of legitimacy is the matter of the Sabbath rest.

The text tells us that his disciples asked Jesus the thorny question of why this man had been born blind. Was it because of something he did? Or was it because his parents had sinned? Jesus rejects the notion that the man's blindness is a punishment for sin, be it his or his parents'. Then he gives the matter a different twist. Rather than dealing with the abstract question of the causes of human suffering, he deals with the concrete reality of this particular man's suffering.

(handwritten margin note: Why would they ask such a question?)

The man's neighbors, and others who had known that he was blind, immediately begin asking questions. Is he really healed? Who healed him? When? Apparently those who ask these questions are somewhat skeptical. Some suggest that the man before them is not the same one that they knew was blind. But the man gives firm witness to what has happened, saying that it was Jesus who told him to go and wash in the pool of Siloam, and that by following those instructions he was healed.

Judge: This passage has many angles that are worthy of consideration. Among others, it is here that Jesus repeats that he is the light of the world. To this we shall return tomorrow.

Today, let us focus our attention on the contrast between the disciples' question and Jesus' response. They want an explanation as to why this evil has happened. Jesus does not give them any apparent reasons, nor does he try to explain to them why there is evil in the world. He simply responds to the man's need.

This is a lesson for us. As we meet the reality of evil, it is quite natural for us to ask questions about its causes, and to seek an explanation for its existence. Why was this man born blind? Why was that little girl killed by a truck? Why are so many children starving to death? We cannot really avoid such questions. Some of them have at least partial answers. For instance, if so many children are starving to death, this probably has something to do with the economic order—or disorder—in which they live, and with the actions of hoarders and others who seek to profit from the existing order. But in many cases there is no real answer, and it is best simply to realize that we cannot explain the mystery of evil. For instance, were we to say that someone is born blind because of a sin committed by his or her parents, we are blaming them for their child's condition, and simply increasing their suffering. In such cases, it is best to reject all explanations that lay blame on someone, as Jesus does in the passage we are studying.

reaction to ? this.

Yet, even though we cannot provide an explanation as to why a particular evil occurs, we can and we must respond to the evil itself. Jesus heals the blind man. In the case of a woman who loses a child to a traffic accident, we can at least try to console and accompany her in her grief. What we must not do is hide behind theoretical or general explanations in order to do nothing about the concrete evil facing us. A long, learned, and profound discussion as to why the man was blind would have been no help to him. Such discussions may well be little more than an excuse not to deal with evil itself.

Act: Look at your own neighborhood. Focus your attention on a particular evil or concrete instance of suffering in your neighborhood. This could be a personal case, such as someone who has lost a loved one; or it could be something affecting the entire community, such as poor schools or lack of public transportation. Write down a list of such evils. Resolve to deal with at least one of them during the coming week. Discuss the matter with others. Write down your reflections and the results of your actions.

Seventh Day: Read John 9:13-41.

See: The people who at first doubted the miracle itself now take the previously blind man to the Pharisees. Once again the man tells the story of what happened. This causes a disagreement among the Pharisees, for some think that only someone who truly comes from God could do such things, while others argue that what Jesus has done is a breach of God's Law. These then try to prove that there has been no miracle. They call the man's parents hoping that they will tell them what actually happened. They answer that the man was indeed blind from birth, but they do not know how he was healed. In any case, they add, their son is a grown man, and quite able to speak for himself. (At this point, John tells us that the man's parents did not wish to testify because they feared being expelled from the synagogue.)

The Pharisees then summon the blind man once again and tell him that Jesus is a sinner who cannot possibly have performed such a miracle. The man answers that he has no idea whether Jesus is a sinner or not; but he is quite certain that he used to be blind, and that now he can see. They insist on questioning him about Jesus, and he finally asks them—with a touch of irony—if their curiosity is an indication that they are considering becoming disciples of Jesus.

The dialogue turns increasingly virulent. Now it is the Pharisees who accuse the man of being a follower of Jesus, while they follow Moses. They are quite certain about Moses, while there are many doubts about Jesus. To this the man responds with another ironic comment: it is strange that these Pharisees, who are supposedly wise, have no idea where Jesus comes from. He then presumes to teach them: since God does not listen to sinners, and Jesus has performed such an unusual miracle, this shows that he must come from God.

The Pharisees now respond by reviling the man. They tell him that he was born in sin—again, a reference to his blindness and its possible explanation—and that therefore he has no right to teach them. As a final act of desperation, they throw him out.

Then Jesus comes to the man and reveals himself to him as the expected "Son of Man." The man worships Jesus, who then comments that he has come for judgment, so that the blind may see, and those who see may be blind. This seems to refer to some of the Pharisees, who ask him if he is indeed referring to them. Jesus answers that it would be better for them to be blind, for then they would at least have an excuse for their sin. But, precisely because they can see, and know what it is that God requires, they are responsible for their own sin.

Judge: Much could be said about this passage. However, since the entire chapter revolves around the theme of seeing and not seeing, and as Jesus here declares himself once again to be "the light of the world," let us reflect on that subject.

"Jesus is the light of the world." We know these words by heart, and we even sing them in some of the hymns we have known since childhood. But let us look more attentively at what this means. To declare that Jesus is the light of the world means at least two things: First, Jesus is the guide we are to follow. In this sense, Jesus is like a lighthouse on a seashore. Ships approaching the coast and seeking a safe haven are guided by the light, and thus avoid reefs and other perils as they enter port. A traveler in the middle of the night sees a light on the horizon and knows that there is a place where he may find shelter. When we declare that Jesus is the light of the world in this sense, we are affirming that Jesus is the guide leading us to the safe haven, to the destination for which we have been created. This is important. The life of discipleship is a constant following of Jesus, taking him as our guide that, like a lighthouse, will help us avoid the shoals and, like a light in the night, will lead us to our final shelter. To say that Jesus is the light is to affirm that we are ready to follow him, and to go wherever he will lead, in the certainty that there is no surer guide.

But there is another sense in which Jesus is the light of the world. Light allows us to see things as they really are. When we were children, sometimes in the middle of the night we saw something that scared us. Perhaps we were in bed, trying to sleep, when we saw a shadow that looked like a monster or an unknown person entering our room. When, after much hesitation, we dared turn on the light, we discovered that what had caused us such fright was something quite ordinary—perhaps some clothes on a chair, with a hat on top, or something like that. Light helps us see things for what they are. Also in this sense is Jesus the light of the world. Jesus lets us see the world for what it is. Without Jesus, when we look at the world, what we see is actually a series of distorted images.

The problem with the Pharisees in today's passage was that they insisted on seeing the world in a way that did not agree with the light of Jesus. They looked upon the blind man as a theological problem: Who sinned? The man or his parents? Was he healed by God, or by powers of evil? In contrast, Jesus sees the blind man as a child of God who is in need, and he responds to that need.

But there is more. As light of the world, Jesus also shows these Pharisees for what they are. He shows it in such a way that the Pharisees ask him if this means that they are blind, and Jesus responds that they are not, for if they were blind they would have an excuse, which they do not have. They have Scripture.

There, and throughout the history of Israel, they may see the world under the light of God; but they refuse to do so. The light of the world not only shows things for what they are; it also shows our own sin and our feeble excuses.

If we truly believe that Jesus is the light of the world, we must see everything under a different light than those who do not know Jesus. Without the light of Jesus, it would seem that other people are either obstacles or opportunities along our way. It would seem that the world is a problem or a challenge to be conquered. Life seems to be nothing but a long race against the rest of humankind, and our goal must be to get ahead of the rest. But under the light of Jesus all these things are different. Other people become children of God whom God loves as much as us, no matter how sinful they may seem. The world and all of nature are God's creation, to be respected as we respect its Creator. Life is an opportunity to serve those who travel through it with us.

Act: Resolve that today you will endeavor to look upon everyone and everything under the light of Jesus. If you see someone, imagine that Jesus is a light shining upon that person, and you will see that person in a radically different way. If you face a problem in your work or at home, shine the same light upon it. Write your reflections and experiences.

For Group Study

Take a copy of today's newspaper to the session. Ask the group to try what has been suggested above, under "Act," but now seeking to apply the light of Jesus to some of the news in the paper. Do not limit your exercise to the first page. Try it on other sections, such as sports, social events, the literary section, pastimes, and others.

W E E K
SIX

First Day: Read John 10:1-6.

See: Although this passage appears at the beginning of a new chapter, it is in fact part of Jesus' response to those who criticized him because he had healed the blind man. Throughout this chapter the prevailing imagery is of a flock and its shepherd. But the use of the image varies.

In this first passage, Jesus presents himself as the true shepherd who enters the fold through the gate. In that society in which raising sheep was a way of life for many people, one always had to be on guard against those who, for various reasons, could harm the flock. Among them were wolves and other animals. In order to protect the flock against them, shepherds would build folds where the sheep were protected—and also kept from straying—by a fence.

Then there were also thieves. Some would jump over the fence and take a lamb that they could easily carry. Or they would jump over the fence, kill a sheep, and carry away the carcass. Since the gate to the fold was usually at a place where the shepherd could see it from the house or the shepherds' camp and there were often people guarding it, thieves would often enter by climbing over the fence.

One of the best helps that shepherds had in protecting the flock was the sheep themselves. If a thief came over the fence, the sheep would flee to one corner and cry out in fear of the intruder. The shepherd, in contrast, was well received by the sheep, for they knew his voice. Therefore, the shepherd could lead the flock into the fold and out of it, and they would follow. Jesus describes himself as this good shepherd whom the sheep recognize because they are his flock.

Judge: This passage reminds us of John 1:11: "He came to his own, and his own received him not." There we were told that the Word through whom all things were made, and who therefore is the universal owner and master of all things, was rejected by the very creatures he made. Here Jesus says that the sheep belong to him, and that for that reason they recognize him. The implication is that the Pharisees who are upset because Jesus healed the blind man are the disobedient ones, the ones who do not recognize their shepherd—or perhaps the thieves who try to pass as shepherds, but who are unable to deceive the flock.

It is important to realize that John tells us that these Pharisees did not understand what Jesus was saying, not because it was unclear, but rather because it was too clear. They did not understand because they did not wish to understand.

We do likewise when we do not like some word from the Lord. We understand it sufficiently well to know that we do not like it, or that it is inconvenient, and then we convince ourselves *example* that we do not understand, thus giving ourselves a reason not to *expand* obey it. Think, for instance, of what Scripture says about the use of money or about caring for the poor and the foreigner. Is that not sufficiently clear? Why, then, do we often claim we do not understand it?

Act: Pray following the first part of a sonnet called "Pastor, que con tus silbos amorosos . . ." by Lope de Vega (1562–1635), and translated by Longfellow:

> SHEPHERD! who with thine amorous, sylvan song
> Hast broken the slumber that encompassed me,
> Who mad'st Thy crook from the accursed tree
> On which Thy powerful arms were stretched so long!
> Lead me to mercy's ever-flowing fountains;
> For Thou my shepherd, guard, and guide shalt be;
> I will obey Thy voice, and wait to see
> Thy feet all beautiful upon the mountains.

Second Day: Read John 10:7-21.

See: Now Jesus shifts the imagery, although still remaining within the context of sheep and their care, for he now says that he is the gate to the fold. By this he means two things. First, those supposed teachers and prophets who do not enter the fold by the gate are not true teachers and prophets, but thieves and bandits. Second, he also uses this image to claim that it is not only the true shepherd who enters by the gate, but also the sheep—as is clear in verse 9: "Whoever enters by me will be saved, and will come in and go out and find pasture." A thief comes only to steal, kill, and destroy, whereas Jesus has come "that they may have life, and have it abundantly."

In verse 11 the use of the imagery shifts once again, and once again the contrast is between the good shepherd, Jesus, who gives his life for the sheep, and the hired hand, who has no real investment in the sheep's welfare. The hired hand does not have an evil intent, like the thief or the bandit; but still, when real danger threatens he runs away because the sheep are not really his. In the end, the result is about the same as if he were a thief, for the wolf comes in and causes as much damage as a thief.

Beginning with verse 14, Jesus leaves aside the comparisons with thieves or hired hands and turns to a positive discussion of his own role as the good shepherd. He is the good shepherd because there is a strong bond between him and the flock, so that they know each other. This relation is parallel to that which exists between Jesus and the Father, who also know each other intimately. It is such a close relationship, that Jesus, the good shepherd, lays down his life for the sheep.

In verse 16, Jesus seems to be quietly declaring that his message is not only for the sheep of the house of Israel, but also for "other sheep that do not belong to this fold." All these sheep, those from the fold of Israel and those from outside, he will join, so that there will be only one flock and only one shepherd.

Finally, Jesus returns to the theme of freely giving up his life for the sheep. He further adds that, after laying down his life, he will take it up again—that is, he will rise from the dead.

As before, at the end of this speech the audience is divided, one side declaring that he has a demon, and the other claiming that the healing of the blind man proves that he does have special powers.

Judge: Jesus speaks of thieves and hired hands. In a way, this is a very harsh word for those of us who claim to have him as our good shepherd, but are not quite ready to follow him. If our shepherd gave his life for our sins so that we might have life abundant, and yet we are ready to follow him only in that which is easy, safe, and comfortable, are we not like the hired hand who takes care of the sheep while there is no danger, but is not ready to take a risk for the sheep or for the owner of the flock? To follow this shepherd means to follow him to the cross. It means following him, not only during the happy times when being a Christian is easy, but also at those times when it becomes difficult, risky, and costly.

The good shepherd gives up his life for the sheep. Jesus has given his life for me. And I still dare to give him only part of my life, trying to hold back a corner for myself! Do you do the same?

Act: Review mentally those dark corners of your life that you still retain for yourself, without surrendering them to Jesus. Think also of the apparently bright corners—your ambitions, your success, your career—that you also withhold.

Finish this session by reading again the lines from Lope de Vega and Longfellow that you read yesterday, as well as the rest of the sonnet:

> Hear, Shepherd Thou who for Thy flock art dying,
> Oh, wash away these scarlet sins, for Thou
> Rejoicest at the contrite sinner's vow.
> Oh, wait! to Thee my weary soul is crying,
> Wait for me: Yet why ask it, when I see,
> With feet nailed to the cross, Thou'rt waiting still for me!

Third Day: Read John 10:22-42.

See: This episode takes place during the Feast of the Dedication, a festival that is mentioned only once in the Bible. This feast—

today called *Hanukkah* among Jews and which takes place near Christmas—celebrated the time when Judas Maccabee purified and rededicated the Temple and its altar, which had been profaned by invaders from Syria.

Once again the Judeans—or rather, the religious leadership in Jerusalem—accost Jesus and demand that he tell them whether he is the Christ, the Messiah, or not. Jesus answers that he has already told them in many ways, but they will not believe. The reason for this, Jesus says, is that they are not part of his flock—and, by implication, that they are not part of the Father's flock. It is not surprising that in response to these words they take up stones to throw at him.

Jesus asks them for which of his good works they are planning to punish him by stoning. Their answer is that they are not stoning him for his works, but for his claim to be equal to God, which is blasphemy. Jesus tells them that his works show that he does indeed come from the Father, and that, if they are not ready to accept his words, they should at least accept and acknowledge his deeds.

Such an answer makes them even angrier, and once again these Judean leaders try to arrest him. But Jesus somehow evades them and crosses over the Jordan, to the desert where John preached before. There people come to him and, seeing that Jesus is fulfilling what John announced, believe in him.

Judge: This story takes us back to the question of the reasons for unbelief. These Judean leaders ask Jesus to tell them openly who he is; but when he does they do not believe him. On the contrary, they try to stone him or at least arrest him.

We too do this sort of thing repeatedly. Thus, sometimes we tell ourselves: "If God were to tell me with absolute clarity what it is I am supposed to do, I would do it." But the truth is that we are often deceiving ourselves. Such attitudes may well be mere excuses not to do what we know we should be doing. Had those Judean leaders believed in Jesus, the consequences would have been quite costly. So, they choose not to believe. At the same time, they do not wish to appear unfair or disbelieving, and so

fair request

they ask Jesus to speak to them clearly. Likewise, when we tell ourselves—or others—that we would do something if God would only tell us clearly that this is what we are to do, we probably already know, or at least have a fairly clear idea, of what it is that God wishes us to do, and we are hiding behind a supposed lack of clarity in order not to do it.

Many years ago, in the youth group in my church, we often read a poem called "Si tú me dices, Ven" by Mexican poet Amado Nervo (1870–1919). The main lines of the poem were: "If you say 'come' I shall leave everything. . . . But tell me clearly. . . ." Now I realize that what we were actually saying by quoting that poem was that we knew quite well that the Lord was saying, "Come," but we were actually postponing obedience by asking for a clearer call. We did not wish to render to the Lord the radical obedience that we knew he demanded, and therefore we hid behind a supposed lack of clarity.

Act: Pray: "Lord, you have called me a thousand times, and a thousand more, and I have responded only half-heartedly, telling myself that if your call were stronger or clearer so too would my obedience be clearer and stronger. Forgive the hardness of my heart. Accept the offering that I now bring to you, my whole life, and make me more obedient to your call. I pray in the name of Jesus, the Good Shepherd who calls me by name. Amen."

Fourth Day: Read John 11:1-16.

See: Today and in the following days we shall be dealing with the resurrection of Lazarus. Today's passage sets the scene for that resurrection. Here we are told that Lazarus became ill, and his sisters Mary and Martha sent word to Jesus, who was still on the other side of the river Jordan. After waiting for two days, Jesus decides to go to Bethany, where the two sisters and their brother live. By then he knows that Lazarus is dead, and he tells this to his disciples.

The decision to go to Bethany is not easy. The religious leadership in Judea had tried to arrest him. That was the reason Jesus had left the area and found refuge across the Jordan. Since Bethany was in Judea, and quite close to Jerusalem, were Jesus to go to his friends' home he would be risking arrest and even death. This was why the disciples tried to dissuade him from going to Bethany.

Finally, when Jesus insists on visiting Lazarus's home in Bethany, his disciples decide to go with him. Note that the one who invites others to follow Jesus, risky as this may be, is Thomas, who would later become famous for his doubts—to the point that even to this day people speak of a "doubting Thomas." The characters in Scripture are much more complex than we sometimes realize.

[margin note: other themes as well as timing]

Judge: As we read this passage, a theme that stands out is solidarity. Jesus practices solidarity with his friends in Bethany. (Further along the story, we shall see him crying over the death of Lazarus.) The disciples, under Thomas's leadership, decide to accompany Jesus to Judea, even though they know that their lives will be endangered. This is closely connected with the theme for the last few days, of Jesus as the good shepherd who gives his life for his sheep.

Solidarity is a fundamental element of Christian life. As Paul says, "If one member suffers, all suffer together with it; if one member is honored, all rejoice together with it" (1 Corinthians 12:26). Furthermore, the term itself, a church "member"—which today we use without even thinking— refers to the church as a body, and to each person as a member of that one body. In that case, one's pain is the pain of all, and one's joy is the joy of all.

But this solidarity must go far beyond mere empathy. It must be shown in action. When someone has to face a difficult or risky situation, it is our responsibility, as members of the same body, to accompany that person as closely as we are able. It is this accompaniment that allows us to experience the church as truly one body.

Act: Try to think of someone you know who is going through difficult times. It could be someone who has lost a loved one, or is unemployed, or is facing a difficult decision. Set aside some time to visit that person, and to show solidarity and companionship.

Fifth Day: Read John 11:17-37.

See: When Jesus arrives at the home in Bethany, Lazarus has been dead for four days. As he approaches, Martha goes out to meet him. She is a woman of faith—even though in Luke 10 Jesus tells Mary that she chose the better part over Martha. She believes that, had Jesus been present, her brother would not have died. A dialogue ensues in which Jesus tells Martha that her brother will rise again, and she says that she knows that this will indeed be the case in the final day. Jesus responds by telling her that he is the resurrection and the life, and that those who believe in him, even if they are dead, will live. Martha reaffirms her faith in him— although quite clearly she is not expecting to see Lazarus rise from the dead.

In this entire dialogue there is an engaging ambiguity, for the conversation seems to take place at two levels. On the one hand, the theme is the final resurrection, and Jesus' final victory over death and over all evil. On the other, the scene is being set for Lazarus's resurrection, not in the last day, but now. Then Mary joins them, and a similar though shorter dialogue follows.

Jesus was moved when he saw the pain of his friends Martha and Mary, and when he saw other people weeping. He was moved to the point of tears.

The reaction of these visitors—probably all Judeans, for Bethany was in Judea, just outside Jerusalem—is double. On the one hand, they noted Jesus' love for this family, and his grief over the death of Lazarus. On the other hand, some felt that if it was true that Jesus had healed the blind man, then he also could have kept Lazarus from dying.

Judge: Death is the horizon of every human life. Although we may not know how or when, we know that we will all die. This life, with its joys and its pains, will come to an end. In a way, the most painful aspect of this fact is not that each of us will die, but that all the people whom we love will also die. Even a small baby in its mother's arms, a baby whose life is just beginning and will in all likelihood extend far beyond ours, will eventually die. In that process we shall have to face the pain of separation, the emptiness of absence, and the ensuing doubts about the meaning of life—and we will have to face them again and again as we watch friends and family die.

Mary and Martha found themselves in that situation. Their brother was dead. And let us not fool ourselves, faith does not shelter us—and did not shelter them—from pain and emptiness. When Jesus arrived, their brother had already been dead for several days, and even so there were still at the house several people who were trying to console the grieving sisters.

The Bible takes death very seriously. We are not told that, simply because we have faith, death is no longer painful. We are told that the final power of death has been overcome; but not its pain or its inevitability. This is why Jesus was moved and wept.

Yet, while the Bible does not claim that the pain of death is no longer there, it does tell us that, no matter how lonely we feel, Jesus is with us in our pain. In this story we see Jesus as one who feels for his friends, and who weeps with them. Too often we imagine Jesus as someone who neither feels nor suffers—a sort of phantom floating in the air. But the Jesus of the Gospels feels, is moved, weeps, and takes the sufferings of his friends very seriously—for these sufferings are similar to his own. In pain and in death, in joy and in life, we are never alone. Jesus is always by our side, suffering or rejoicing with us. And, since Jesus accompanies us in our suffering, we must also accompany others in their suffering.

Act: Review what you resolved yesterday about how you would practice solidarity with someone in a difficult situation. Have you done it? If not, make sure you do it today. Try to make this a daily practice.

Sixth Day: Read John 11:38-44.

See: Today's passage is the climax of this entire story. As was customary, Lazarus's tomb was a cave that had been sealed with a stone. Jesus orders that the tomb be opened, but Martha objects that since Lazarus has been dead for four days, there would be the stench of death. But Jesus insists, and the tomb is finally opened. At that point, Jesus thanks the Father for having heeded his call—adding that this is said aloud so that those who hear these words will believe that he does have a special relationship with the Father—and he calls Lazarus out of the tomb. Lazarus does come out, still wrapped in the cloth in which they had placed him in the sepulcher, and Jesus tells those present to unbind Lazarus and let him go.

Judge: It is surprising that, after such a long introduction in the earlier part of the chapter, the miracle itself is told in just a few lines. The reason for this is that the purpose of the entire chapter is to show the glory of God and Jesus' power over death. Since this has already been presented in various ways in the preceding verses, all that remains to be said is that Jesus did raise Lazarus from among the dead. John presents him as confirming by this action all that he has just said about himself, his relationship with the Father, and his power over death.

True for all of X's healings

On the other hand, let us not forget that eventually Lazarus did die. His resurrection, as told by John in this passage, was not the final resurrection that Martha discussed with Jesus. Lazarus died, was raised, and died again to await the final resurrection. What then is the significance of his resurrection? It is an indication of the manner in which all believers are to live: as those who have already left death behind—not because they will not die, but because Jesus is the resurrection and the life, and in him we have life and resurrection.

Imagine Lazarus's life after his death and resurrection. Do you think he could go on living as before? Certainly not. From the moment of the events told in John 11, Lazarus would live as someone who has already died, and therefore is no longer afraid of death. In a way, the time he now has is like a bonus, an unexpected gift. Two things will be different for him: first, he will no longer fear death; second, he will experience a new sense of freedom, as someone who no longer has to affirm his own life.

Some years ago, I had an experience that I could somehow compare with Lazarus's resurrection. For three hours I was on board a plane that was completely out of control, and it seemed almost certain that we would all die. In a way, I did die. When the plane finally managed to land, it was like a resurrection. Since then, all these extra years I have lived have been like an unexpected gift from God—much like a bonus. Why should I fear death, when I have already once faced death, and God returned my life? What that experience taught me is what every believer should know: life is a gift of God from beginning to end. We are free to live it without fear of death, for death also will be subjected to our Lord.

Act: Imagine that you die tonight and that tomorrow you return from the dead. Do you think such an experience would change your life? Write your reflections. Now consider this: For those who believe in Christ, it is as if we have already died and risen with him. Therefore, what you have just written could well be a guide or pattern for your present life. Write down any further reflections.

Seventh Day: Read John 11:45-57.

See: This passage shows that the resurrection of Lazarus, like the rest of Jesus' deeds and teachings, had a political impact, and that it was this impact that eventually took Jesus to the cross.

In order to understand this it is important to remember that Judea was part of the Roman Empire. In many ways, the Romans were relatively benign in their use of power over subjected nations. As long as tributes were paid and there was no disorder and no rebellion—which were matters of supreme importance for the Empire—its subjects could enjoy a measure of autonomy.

This was probably one of the reasons why that empire was so successful. Up to that time, most great empires had sought to impose their ideas, their religion, and their uses on all conquered populations. But for the most part, the Roman Empire was content with the economic and political benefits that it drew from its vast possessions, and was not overly concerned over having all its subjects follow the same religion or the same customs.

The Judean leaders knew that the Empire was powerful enough to crush the entire people of Israel if they dared reclaim their independence, or if there was any sort of disorder that might interrupt the flow of taxes to Rome. At the same time, there still was among the people a strong nationalist feeling and hope. Some of its most extreme elements, the zealots, believed that God would deliver them from the Roman yoke, just as God had delivered Israel from Egypt's yoke.

It was this popular sentiment that caused grave concern to the religious leaders, who knew that if someone arose who could somehow lead the people in their quest for freedom there might well be a rebellion. The result of such events would be the end of Judea as a nation. The Temple, as well as Jerusalem itself, would probably be destroyed by the Romans—as did happen later, in the year 70.

In a way, the desire of these leaders to silence Jesus had a patriotic motivation. And, since in the history of Israel the sense of nationality had always been joined to the religion of Israel, the attempt to silence Jesus also had a religious motivation. But this was not the only reason why the religious leaders of the Judeans wished to be rid of Jesus. His attacks on the false and stringent religiosity of the Pharisees and the teachers of the Law, his healing of persons on the Sabbath, and his acceptance and even commendation of people whom the religious leaders considered sinners, were all reasons for enmity against him.

All these motivations came together to create an organized opposition to Jesus. The leadership in Judea resisted the preaching and the miracles of Jesus. But that leadership was also very much afraid that if Jesus' popularity grew and a riot or rebellion ensued, they would not be able to bring the people to their senses. There was always the danger that the people would follow this preacher from Galilee whom some were beginning to call "King of the Jews." Were such a thing to happen, Roman intervention would be swift and terrible. Therefore, for the good of the nation and of its religion, Jesus had to be destroyed.

Judge: What does all of this have to do with us? We are certainly not conspiring against Jesus to protect our nation or its freedom. Nor do we say that it is better for Jesus to be crucified because we find his preaching troublesome. It would seem that we have nothing in common with Caiaphas and the other Judean leaders. But let us not declare ourselves innocent so glibly. Are there not times when we subordinate the message and teaching of Jesus to our own personal or collective convenience? As members of the church, we are part of the people of God. For some of us, the church is just as important as Israel was for Caiaphas. Are there times when we place the prestige or the convenience of the church above the teachings of Jesus?

Consider an example. We all know about the enormous tragedy of hunger and starvation in various parts of the world. As Christians, we feel we must do something. With that in mind, we try to learn more about the issues involved, so that we may do something about it. We may then reach the conclusion that part of the problem is that in the richer countries, including ours, there is a high level of consumption of sugar, coffee, imported flowers, and other such products of little nutritional value. We learn, for instance, that in order to produce the sugar we consume—and which contributes to an epidemic of obesity in our country—large expanses of land must be devoted to growing sugar cane. We also learn that much of the beef for our fast-food chains is produced overseas, in lands previously devoted to cereals and other food crops for local consumption. As a result, people in those countries now have to buy imported food, which is much more expensive and which the poor cannot afford.

The immediate reaction of many Christians to this reality is to consider a campaign, for instance, to lower the consumption of sugar in our own communities. We are further encouraged by the fact that doctors and medical research tell us that people in our country are consuming too much sugar, and that this imperils their health. But then we learn that one of the main ways in which people consume sugar—often scarcely noticing it—is in soft drinks, and that one of the most popular soft drinks in our community is produced by a company that over the years has provided much support for the church—and perhaps still does. There may be people in our congregation who hold stock in that company. It is even possible that our denomination also owns such stock—perhaps some of it supporting its pension system or its educational institutions. It is obvious that if the campaign we have been considering gains momentum, many friends and even members of the church will be upset. <u>In short, if we do what our conscience tells us we should do, we may be creating problems both for ourselves and for the church.</u>

What do we do in such cases? Isn't it true that now Caiaphas and his companions do not seem as despicable as they did at first?

Act: Think of some need in your community. Now write it down on your notebook: "A problem in our community is that _____, and our church should _____." You may repeat this several times if there is more than one need that comes to mind.

If your church is doing what you think it should do in response to that particular need, pray thanking God that this is the case.

If not, write: "But our church does not because _____." Discuss what you have written with other members of the church.

For Group Study

Focus your attention on a particular problem or need in your community, and complete the first of the blanks in the sentences suggested above. Then invite the group to discuss how they would fill the other blanks.

W E E K
SEVEN

First Day: Read John 12:1-8.

See: The story in today's passage is often mixed and confused with other similar stories in the Gospels. Thus it is often said that this was Mary Magdalene, who supposedly was a great sinner. But there is no mention here of this woman being particularly sinful. Nor is the woman Mary Magdalene, but Mary of Bethany, the sister of Martha and Lazarus, a friend and sometimes hostess to Jesus and his disciples.

The story in John is brief and clear: Mary uses some very costly perfume to anoint Jesus. Considering this to be an outrageous waste, Judas criticizes her, declaring that it would have been better to sell the perfume and give the proceeds to the poor. John tells us that Judas did not say this because he was really concerned for the poor, but rather because he was in charge of the group's funds, and was using them for his own purposes. Thus, John seems to imply that Judas thought that if all that money were given to him to turn over to the poor, some would stick to his fingers.

On the other hand, Judas's comment, that it would have been much better to sell the perfume and give the money to the poor, had a very practical and reasonable dimension. Jesus himself had criticized those who employed vast resources in religious ostentation, but did not look to the needs of the poor and the oppressed.

Where Judas erred was in thinking that all occasions are to be measured with the same practical and calculating attitude. When every action is calculated, we risk missing the unique times that demand a unique response. In this case, Mary wishes to celebrate the glorious and welcome presence of Jesus in her home. It is time for joyful extravagance—even wasteful extravagance. So, she joyfully wastes the expensive perfume in anointing Jesus.

Jesus' response to the recriminations of Judas is important. He declares that Mary, even without knowing it, has anointed him for his death. This is a unique moment, one in which extravagance is appropriate. And in any case, Jesus adds, the poor will always be there, whereas Jesus himself will soon leave their company.

Judge: Unfortunately, these words of Jesus at the end of the passage have often been employed as an excuse for doing nothing about poverty and the plight of the poor. Sometimes it is said that according to Jesus poverty is part of God's design for humankind, and that therefore we should simply accept it as we accept God's will in other matters.

But what Jesus means is exactly the opposite. Now that he is present there, before Mary, and preparing to face death, it is good to be extravagant in honoring him. Later, when he will no longer be physically present, the poor will still be among us, so that on their behalf we may act as extravagantly as Mary did with Jesus. If, as Jesus says in Matthew 25, when we clothe the naked we clothe him, and when we feed the hungry we feed him, then in the presence of the naked and the hungry we must act with a liberal extravagance similar to Mary's in the presence of Jesus.

Act: Find out what programs your local church or your denomination has developed to serve the needy. Make a special gift to one of those programs. Do it in honor of Jesus and of the poor.

Second Day: Read John 12:9-11.

See: This is a very brief passage—only three verses. Jesus is still at the home of his friends in Bethany, and many "Jews"—that is, Judeans—come to see him, but also to see Lazarus. One may well imagine the commotion produced by the news that there was a man in Bethany who, after having been dead four days, had returned to life. This means that many came simply out of curiosity. But others, upon seeing Lazarus—and perhaps hearing his testimony as well as that of his sisters—came to believe.

This event causes great chagrin among the religious leaders of Judea, who feel slighted and deserted, and therefore decide that it is necessary to kill, not only Jesus, but also Lazarus. John does not tell us whether they eventually managed to kill Lazarus or not. (There is an ancient legend that claims that Lazarus and his two sisters were put in a leaky boat and shoved out to sea, in the expectation that they would drown. But they reached Cyprus, where Lazarus later became a bishop.)

Judge: These three brief verses give us a glimpse at the depths of human evil. The chief priests, who supposedly were devoted to the service of truth and justice, plan to destroy a man whose only fault is that he has come back from the dead. As we have seen, they justified this sort of action on the basis of the precarious political situation of Judea. They feared that if the rumor grew that there was a new King of the Jews, there would be an uprising, and Rome would respond by destroying what little autonomy Judea still had.

All of this serves as a warning to us. It is quite easy, when we wish to do something that is not right, to find a way to justify such a course of action, and to do this to such a point that our conscience is satisfied. The Spanish conquistadores and other European settlers killed thousands upon thousands of the original inhabitants of the Americas, and many of them were quite convinced that in so doing they were serving God—while also becoming rich with the possessions and the lands of the Indians. The inquisitors who incarcerated and tortured so many people, and who put quite a few of them to death, were doing this in order to defend the integrity of the faith—even though many of those whom they tortured or killed were their own personal enemies, and their possessions were confiscated and often put in the hands of the inquisitors. Even today, there are those who have convinced themselves that they are serving God when they place a bomb in an abortion clinic—even though, in fact, they are venting their own hatred and anger.

Act: Review and make a mental list of your activities and actions during a certain time (for instance, during this past week). What were the reasons for your actions? Did you try to justify actions or attitudes that in truth had no justification? Write your reflections.

Were your intentions always honorable?

Third Day: Read John 12:12-19.

See: We now come to Jesus' triumphal entry into Jerusalem. According to John's telling of the story, Jesus had already been in the Holy City several times, and had already cleansed the Temple. Now he had spent some time in Bethany, where he had gone in order to raise Lazarus from the dead. (Remember that a few days ago we noted that Jesus knew that some people in Judea sought to kill him, and that for this reason he had left the area and gone to the other side of the Jordan. Now that he has returned because of the death of Lazarus, he seems to be in no hurry to leave Judea.)

Hebrew meaning "save"

The crowds shouted "Hosanna!" as a word of welcome greeting. Although today in church it is often used as a word of praise, it was originally a word of pleading. It welcomed the one who arrived, and in doing so, called for the fulfillment of the promises. If we take this into account, we may begin to understand why the crowd that shouted "Hosanna!" did not oppose the crucifixion of Jesus. (As we shall see, in the Gospel of John it is not actually the crowd, but the religious leaders of Judea, that shout, "Crucify him!") What the crowd shouted was a plea, a petition. They wanted Jesus to restore the throne of David. They wanted to be freed from their subjection to the Romans. When Jesus did not fulfill these expectations—at least, not immediately—there seemed to be no reason to follow him any more.

The main reason why the crowd shouts "Hosanna!" is that they have heard of the resurrection of Lazarus. This Jesus who has power over death must certainly have the power necessary to restore the throne of David. At any rate, while the crowd

New believers

shouts, not all rejoice. The Pharisees, or at least some among them, see Jesus' triumphal entry as an indication that more drastic measures are required.

Judge: In a way, the crowds that shout "Hosanna!" have faith. They are sincere. The problem is not their lack of sincerity or their lack of faith. The problem is that they misunderstand that faith. They trust Jesus to give them certain things—in this case, political freedom. If Jesus does not deliver on these expectations, they will find another savior in whom to lay their trust, and from whom to ask what they wish.

Unfortunately, even today there is much of that sort of faith. There are those who believe because they expect Jesus to heal them from some illness. They then look for Jesus in a particular church where such expectations are fostered. If they are not healed, they simply try another church. And another . . . And another . . . If at some point they are told that a medicine man of some sort, or a spiritualist medium, may be able to heal them, they will lay their trust on that person.

True faith involves much more than merely receiving what we desire. In fact, it is very difficult to distinguish between true faith and love. Whoever loves God and trusts in God, without setting conditions or demands, has true faith.

Act: Pray: "Thanks, Lord, for your presence in my life. Without you, my life would not be what it is. In fact, without you I would not exist at all. I thank you for my life; and all I ask of you is that you remain forever present in my life, and increase my love and faith in you. Amen."

Fourth Day: Read John 12:20-26.

See: These events are placed immediately after the triumphal entry into Jerusalem. One may well imagine that the disciples were joyful and enthusiastic, for finally their Master was receiving the praise that he deserved. But things change quite rapidly, for Jesus begins to speak of the suffering, death, and resurrection that await him.

Some "Greeks" who had come to Jerusalem for the Passover show an interest in meeting Jesus. They are not really Greeks, but rather Greek-speaking Jews, whom the Jews from Palestine often called "Greeks." By then, there were many Jews living in distant countries who no longer spoke Hebrew or Aramaic—the language that was then spoken in Judea—but rather Greek, which was the *lingua franca* or common language of much of the Roman Empire. Such Greek-speaking Jews were often called "Greeks" to distinguish them from the "Hebrews"—that is, Palestinian Jews who still spoke the language of their ancestors. Thus, although these people who come to Jesus spoke Greek, they are actually Jews, and for that reason have come to Jerusalem for Passover.

It is apparently due to this linguistic difference that they approach Philip, who is from Bethsaida in Galilee, an area where such Jewish "Greeks" abounded. It is interesting to note that both Philip and Andrew, the other disciple who serves as an intermediary, have Greek names. (The names of the other disciples, Simon, James, John, et al., are Semitic in origin.)

When the Master learns that these "Greeks" are asking for him, he declares that his "hour" has come. We are not told why; but apparently Jesus is well aware that the more his fame increases the more his enemies will feel the urgency to destroy him. Jesus then explains that he has to die and be raised again. He uses as an example a grain of wheat that bears much fruit, precisely because it falls on the ground and dies. He then adds that the way of the cross is not only for himself, but also for all his followers. Those who really wish to follow him will take a path that leads to suffering, the cross, and eventual glory.

Judge: From the very beginning, even before the death and resurrection of Jesus, it was clear that his message had to cross cultural and linguistic barriers. In this case, we note that it happened by using some of the gifts and connections of two of the disciples. Philip and Andrew, because of their upbringing, could serve as bridges for these "Greeks" to come to Jesus.

We live in an increasingly multicultural society. Not only in the United States, but also throughout the world, people are on the move. Cultures meet, clash, and mingle. In practically all our churches, we have people of different backgrounds and connections. The church is called to use those connections to cross cultural and other bridges, and to proclaim the gospel throughout all the world and in all its cultures—not only overseas, but also in our local communities, where more and more cultures are present every day. Are we using these opportunities to bring others to Jesus?

Act: Think about your community, your neighbors, the people who work in your stores, in your factories and farms. <u>What are some of the different groups in the community</u>? Consider what your church is doing—or not doing—to reach these various people. What else could it do? Do you yourself have opportunities to cross such bridges? How are you using them? Write down your reflections, and then share them with others in your church.

Fifth Day: Read John 12:27-36.

See: Although Jesus is ready to offer his life, this in no way diminishes his pain and anguish. On the contrary, he declares that his soul is troubled, but in spite of that, he will not avoid the suffering that awaits him. A voice from heaven confirms this mission of Jesus. Only some understand its meaning; others say that it was a clap of thunder. Note that this heavenly confirmation is similar to the one that took place at the baptism of Jesus. Once again we see what we have noted before, that a miracle does not necessarily lead to faith. In this case, while some hear the voice, others explain it away as a natural and fairly common phenomenon, thunder.

Jesus declares that the voice is a testimony from God, so that those who hear it may believe. His own presence is a judgment on the world. By the incarnation, death, and resurrection of Jesus, "the ruler of this world will be driven out."

The title "Son of Man," which the crowd employs here and which Jesus claims for himself elsewhere, referred to the expectation of a celestial being who would come to save Israel. It is not an affirmation of the humanity of Jesus, but rather of his connection with the hopes of Israel, and of his having come from heaven with a messianic mission. This is why those who hear him have difficulties with the notion that the Son of Man will suffer. But Jesus insists on that point.

The final verses in our text return to the theme of Jesus as the light of the world, which we have seen elsewhere in the Gospel of John. What Jesus says here is that, since he is that light, the time to walk is now, when the light is present.

Judge: The death and resurrection of Jesus are not isolated events with no connection to each other, to the rest of his life, or to the life of the world. Jesus himself says that it is impossible to rise with him without also first dying with him. As Christians, we are called to give up our lives. We live in a society in which people are expected to look after their own interests and their own affairs and to "get ahead"—even at the expense of others. It would seem that success in life consists in enjoying as much as possible and suffering as little as possible. But Jesus tells us otherwise. We are each to look after the concerns of all, and especially after God's concerns; we are to give up our lives in service to others; we are to live in order to die in Christ. Certainly, we are to look after our own health and our own life; but not as if they were our own, for they too belong to Christ.

What signs have you given today, that your life actually belongs to Christ, and therefore also to all others who may be in need?

Finally, remember that what is true of individual Christians is also true of the church as a whole. The purpose of the church is not the success of the church itself. The church, just as every individual believer, must also be ready to give up its life in order to find it. A Christian whose life is centered on himself or herself is not a faithful Christian. A church whose life is centered on itself is not a faithful church.

Act: List some of the ways you can devote your life to the service of others. List some of the ways your church could show the world that it is willing to die for the community in which it stands, and that its purpose is not to serve itself. Share this second list with your pastor, and with other members and leaders of the church.

Sixth Day: Read John 12:37-43.

See: This passage functions much like an interlude. It does not say a word about anything that Jesus did. Actually, all we are told about him is that "he departed and hid from them." Here John tells us rather about the reactions of the people and of their leaders to the preaching and deeds of Jesus. In general, that reaction is disbelief. John explains such disbelief as the fulfillment of the prophecies of Isaiah, who spoke repeatedly of the unbelief of the people.

But there is more. Some of those who believe, "even of the authorities," do not dare say so for fear of the Pharisees, who will expel them from the synagogue if they are found to be followers of Jesus. It is interesting to note that John does not attribute this motivation to the entire crowd, but specifically to some of the rulers, that is, to some people from the higher echelons of society. For such people, to be expelled from the synagogue would be a great disgrace. Therefore, they do not dare declare that they believe in Jesus, even when in fact they do.

John explains this in the last verse of the passage: "for they loved human glory more than the glory that comes from God." In other words, for these important people in society being expelled from the synagogue—and therefore from their position of respect—would be too high a price for believing and following Jesus.

Judge: What John tells us here about these people in authority we see often enough in our own day. For instance, quite often when a church begins making significant inroads into the poorer neighborhoods of a town, and people from such neighborhoods begin joining, some of its more respectable members begin to drift away. They fear for their prestige. They are afraid that people will associate them with others who do not dress as well, do not hold important positions in society, are not very highly educated, or speak with a foreign accent. If, on the other hand, it becomes known that there is a church where important people gather, quite often other people of high standing in society begin to join—and even some whose ambition is to have such standing follow suit. If, because of the social and educational standing of its members, a church has an impressive choir, a beautiful building, and a famous pastor, some people are quite eager to join it who would not join a poorer church.

Is this attitude much different from the attitude of those rulers and important people who did not dare declare their faith in Jesus because they loved human glory more than the glory that comes from God?

But let us think not only about such persons. Let us think also about ourselves. Are we ready to be seen with all sorts of people, to invite them to our church? Are we ready to sit with people who do not dress well, who do not have what we do, or who do not smell as we do? If not, could it be that we too love human glory more than the glory that comes from God?

Act: Resolve that during this coming week you will invite—or even better, bring—someone to your church whom the rest of the community might consider less worthy or less important than your typical church member. Sit next to that person. Make him or her feel welcome. Introduce her or him to your friends.

Seventh Day: Read John 12:44-50.

See: John does not tell us when or where these events took place. (The Greek particle that the NRSV translates as "then" is not really that strong. It does not necessarily mean right there and then. It is more a way of starting a new point in a narrative, much like our English "so.") For this reason, some interpreters suggest that John is not referring to a specific event, but rather to the general response of Jesus to the incredulity of some, and to the hesitation of others in declaring their faith in him. At any rate, today's passage is a series of assertions of Jesus about himself.

The first theme of these assertions is the relationship between Jesus and the Father. The second theme is the consequences that will follow from believing or from not believing in him.

As to his relationship with the Father, in this passage Jesus reaffirms one of the central threads in the Gospel of John: his unity with the Father. Believing in him also means believing in the Father. (Which implies, although he does not say it in so many words, that those who do not believe in him do not believe in the Father either.) Furthermore, that relationship is so close that whoever sees Jesus also sees the Father.

This reference to "seeing" leads into the subject of light. We are told once more that Jesus is the light of the world. Furthermore, he is not only the light of the world; he is light itself and has come to the world to illumine those who believe in him—so that they "should not remain in darkness."

Then attention shifts to the consequences of believing and not believing in Jesus. In verses 47 and 48, Jesus declares that if someone does not believe in him, it is not even necessary for him to judge that person, since that person will be judged by the very words of Jesus that he or she did not accept. And since Jesus is the truth and his words are true, to reject Jesus and his words is to reject truth and live in falsehood—which in itself is already condemnation.

Finally, the circle is completed, as Jesus returns to the subject of his relationship with the Father. The reason why the word of Jesus is true and powerful is that it comes from the Father. Therefore, just as whoever has seen Jesus has seen the Father, so also whoever rejects Jesus rejects the Father.

Judge: Throughout this passage, Jesus speaks in terms of two alternatives, with no other options in between. One may believe in him or not believe in him. It is possible to walk in light or to remain in darkness. What is not possible is to be somewhere between these two alternatives. I cannot believe in Jesus and not follow him. I cannot follow him halfway. I cannot believe in him and not believe in the Father. I cannot believe in the Father and not in him. I cannot reject him and hope that this will not bring judgment upon myself. I cannot accept some of his words and not others; some of his commands and not others; some of his claims and not others.

In our relationship to Jesus, only two words are possible: yes or no. Jesus calls for a total commitment. A partial commitment is no commitment at all. This does not mean that Christians have to be perfect; but it does mean that our commitment has to be real and all-encompassing.

Act: Upon completing the studies for this week, we have passed the midpoint in our three months with John. It is therefore a good time to take inventory of where we are, how far we have gone, and how far we have to go.

Make a list in your notebook of various areas of your life, such as work, family, church, money, politics, study, or sports. Think about each item you listed for a moment. In which of these is your discipleship most advanced? In which is it lagging? As you find yourself lacking in some of these areas, write a note about how your discipleship in that particular area could be better.

End the session with a time of prayer, confessing your shortcomings and asking the Lord to make you a better disciple.

For Group Study

In this passage there are several subjects or themes that are central to the Gospel of John, such as: the relationship of Jesus and the Father; light and darkness; judgment; and so forth.

Invite the group to make a list of these themes. Write them down on newsprint. Now ask the group to review what they remember about where these themes appear in the Gospel of John, and what is said about them. Since this is a review, focus attention on the part of the Gospel that we have already studied—but allow people to speak also of what they know of the chapters that we have not studied yet.

WEEK
EIGHT

First Day: Read John 13:1-9.

See: These events take place at the same supper where Jesus will announce Judas's betrayal to his disciples—which we will study the day after tomorrow. During the supper, Jesus disrobes, girds himself with a towel, and begins to wash his disciples' feet. In those days of open sandals and dusty roads, it was customary to welcome and recognize the value of guests by washing their feet and anointing their beard. For a tired traveler, with aching feet still burning from the heat of the road, that action provided welcome relief. Usually, it was a servant who washed the feet of guests, particularly if the host was relatively well-to-do. If the host had no servants, then he did it himself. At any rate, washing the feet of another was considered both an act of hospitality and a kindness.

In this case, the disciples would naturally be shocked at having Jesus wash their feet. After all, he was the teacher and they the disciples. It would be more appropriate to have them wash his feet. This is why Peter is uncomfortable and asks: "Lord, are you going to wash my feet?" To this Jesus answers: "Unless I wash you, you have no share with me." And at these words Peter, in his usual dramatic fashion, offers to have not only his feet washed, but also his hands and his head.

Judge: When Jesus washes the feet of the disciples, this signals two things. It is first a sign of humility. To this we will return tomorrow. But it is also a sign of his readiness to wash away sin, to cleanse the human heart. It is for this second reason that Jesus tells Peter that if he will not allow himself to be washed, he will have no part with Jesus.

Christian life requires purity and commitment. God does not like filth. What is not clean cannot be presented before the throne of the Most High. But, thanks be to God, it is not a matter of washing ourselves—which we could never do properly. Jesus offers to cleanse Peter and any others who would ask him so to do.

The problem is that quite often, like Peter, we insist on washing ourselves. We know that we have sinned, and we insist on making ourselves clean by punishing ourselves, by making a better effort not to sin, or by trying to undo whatever evil we have done. We should certainly make every effort not to sin again, and also to undo the results of our evil. But this is not what renders us clean. What purifies us is Jesus himself. To try to become clean by our own means and effort is another way of rejecting Jesus, no matter how holy it might seem. In the end, we must come to the point of saying, like Peter: "Lord, not my feet only, but also my hands and my head!"

Act: Pray: "Lord, you know how often I am not as pure as you would wish. You also know how often I act as if I could cleanse myself. Forgive my impurity. Forgive my pride in trying to cleanse myself by my own effort. Wash me Lord, and I shall be clean! Amen."

Second Day: Read John 13:10-17.

See: There are throughout this chapter a number of references to Judas's betrayal—a betrayal that will become clearer in tomorrow's passage. In yesterday's text, there was a passing reference to it in verse 2. Today's passage begins by referring to this once again.

But the central point of the passage occurs further on. After washing his disciples' feet, Jesus asks them: "Do you know what I have done to you?" He then explains that if he, their Master and Lord, has washed their feet, they are to do likewise among themselves. Since servants are not greater that their masters, they should not consider themselves above such menial and humble tasks. For the disciples to feel that washing each other's feet is too humble a task, and to therefore refuse to do it, would be to consider themselves more important than their own Lord, who had washed their feet.

Judge: If in truth we are servants and followers of that Jesus who washed his disciples' feet, we too must follow the path of humble service. There is no form of service that is too humble for a Christian, for to think so would be to consider ourselves above our Master. Furthermore, just as he washed his disciples' feet without waiting to be asked, so too are we to look around us and see who needs a service we can render.

Up to this point, the lesson of this story about foot washing seems crystal clear. But the truth is that it is much easier to understand this lesson than to apply it in our own lives. We all know that we are to serve others, and that we are to do this humbly. But in actual practice things are not so simple. When someone crosses our path, we do not even pause to think about what she or he might need, for we are too busy with our own concerns, and this other person is just an obstacle on our way. If we do somehow come to recognize her or his need, we easily convince ourselves that what we are doing is more important. And then, in those—often few—cases when we see a need and do something about it, we expect praise and honor. Even when we act humbly, we get upset that others do not recognize our great humility—even in our humility, we are proud!

This is why Jesus tells us that we are in need of being washed by him. Pride and egotism are so deeply rooted in our very being, that we cannot simply tell ourselves, "from now on I shall be humble and serve others."

All this is of one piece. Our resistance to serving others and our pride when we are of service to someone are both indications that we need the Lord to cleanse us. It does not suffice to tell ourselves that we are prideful and egotistic, but we can do nothing about it. In fact, this is just another excuse for continuing along our old paths. Rather it is a matter of serving others in humility, and at the same time asking the Lord to cleanse us from these and other sins, as we recognize the pride and egotism still present in us.

Act: Review your life and your deeds during the past week and make an inventory of the times you have served another. Have you done so humbly, without demanding or expecting a reward? What motivated your action? What resulted from it? Have you felt the presence of the Lord, cleansing away your sin?

In the days to come, keep a journal in which you write down the acts of service you have performed. At the end of each day, offer all of it up to the Lord and ask for a spirit of greater service and humility.

Third Day: Read John 13:18-30.

See: This passage also occurs during the same supper when Jesus washed the feet of his disciples. He now declares openly what he had hinted at before: one of his disciples will betray him. In order to understand this, we must remember that earlier his enemies had decided to arrest Jesus and have him executed, but did not dare do so in a public place, for fear of causing a riot. Thus, they needed someone to take them to Jesus when he was alone or only with his closest disciples. This is what Judas agreed to do.

Upon hearing the harsh announcement that one of them would betray their Master, all were perturbed, and Peter directed John, who was next to Jesus, to ask him who it would be. This is what John did, apparently in a low voice, for otherwise the rest of the narrative does not make sense. Jesus told him that it would be the one to whom he would give the soaked bread. Upon giving this bread to Judas, Jesus told him to hurry up and do what he had decided to do. The other disciples did not know what Jesus meant, because they had not heard the conversation between John and Jesus. Since it was Judas who held the purse for the group, on seeing him leave, the others thought that he was going to make a purchase for the feast, or perhaps to give some money to the poor.

Judge: The name of Judas has passed into history as a name of infamy. So much so, that this name, which until then had been borne by several important leaders in the history of Israel, soon fell into disuse, and today is frequently used as a synonym for "traitor." What we often forget is that Judas, like the rest of the disciples, had left his former life in order to follow Jesus, and up to that time had apparently been a faithful follower. The other disciples seem to have trusted him enough to put him in charge of their finances. Yet in spite of all that, he became a traitor.

This means that each one of us, no matter how devoted to the Lord, must be always watchful in order not to fall (see 1 Corinthians 10:12). It is easy to blame Judas for his actions, as if he were a particularly evil person. It is more difficult—and more important—to see him as an example of what any one of us could become were it not for God's grace. This story calls us to be constantly watchful so that we may not fall into temptation. And this is one of the reasons why a disciplined life of devotion and study of Scripture is so important.

Act: Pray: Lord, you know how often I have denied or betrayed you, how often I have forgotten you, how often I have failed to witness to you. Sometimes I was held back by fear, sometimes by convenience, and sometimes by reasons I don't know. It is so easy to deny you! I ask that you give me the strength and the courage to be a faithful witness to all you have done for me. I pray you, Lord, leave me not! Amen.

Fourth Day: Read John 13:31-35.

See: Now that Judas is gone, Jesus speaks of the future, of the time after his death and resurrection. He is no longer speaking of the betrayal, but of what will come after that. Even though what is immediately facing him is the cross, Jesus speaks of his glorification. In other words, the cross is the path leading to resurrection and glorification. But that very glorification implies that Jesus will no longer be present among his disciples—at least not in the physical and visible way he has been present until this time. This is why he begins to prepare them for the time when he will no longer be with them.

As part of that preparation, he gives them a "new commandment": to love each other. This is not new in the sense of being unexpected, for Jesus had already said that the two greatest commandments refer to the love of God and to the love of neighbor. It is new in the sense that the disciples will find themselves in a new situation, and this commandment should guide them in that situation. When the Lord is no longer with them, the disciples are to love each other as Jesus has loved them. This love will be an important part of their witness before the world, for when the world sees how the disciples love one another it will know that they are true followers of Jesus.

Judge: When Jesus announced his departure to his disciples, the first thing he commanded them to do was to love each other. If we call ourselves followers of Jesus, this commandment is also for us. This is the very first clause of Jesus' guidelines for Christian life.

And yet, it is precisely at this point that the church has most often failed to give faithful witness. Sometimes there are within the church fights and prejudices that are at least as bad as those that exist in other places. Sometimes we fight over unimportant things. For example, Mr. Smith says that the committee should have five members, and Mrs. James says that there should be seven. Each insists on his or her position, and the disagreement results in permanent ill feelings. Joe did not greet Jane. Harry helped paint the annex, but no one thanked him for it. All these things, and many more, result in strife within the church. And then we marvel that the world does not believe! What can we do in our own local congregation to promote and practice love? What can we do in our denomination? In the worldwide church?

Act: Write down your reflections. Seek other people with similar concerns. Resolve to take whatever steps are necessary so that there will be a more loving atmosphere in your church.

Fifth Day: Read John 13:36-38.

See: Peter's question follows up on the conversation we studied yesterday. Jesus has just told his disciples that where he is going they cannot follow, but Peter wants to know where he is going. Jesus responds without clarifying the mystery, insisting that for the time being Peter cannot follow him, but will later.

Apparently Peter thinks that Jesus is going to a dangerous

place, perhaps to face the powerful in Jerusalem and to claim the throne for himself. That is why he insists on following him, and even offers to sacrifice his life for him. But Jesus, who knows the flaws of human nature, tells him that before the cock crows— that is, before daybreak—he will deny Jesus three times.

Judge: The passage is brief, but well deserving of profound reflection. Two days ago we studied the betrayal by Judas, and we were warned not to imagine that we are too strong or firm in our faith, for even Judas seems to have been a good disciple for some time. But, having said that, it is easy for us still to think, deep down, that we are better than Judas. Certainly, we would never act as he did! We know that Jesus is the Lord of life and of death, and therefore we will never deny him, even if our life were at risk! With such thoughts, we are quite likely not to heed the warning of Judas's example.

But things change when we see what happened to Peter, one of the very first disciples of Jesus. He is so firm that Jesus has nicknamed him "stone" or "rock." He has been close to Jesus from the very beginnings of his ministry. He left his boat and his nets to follow Jesus. Jesus visited Peter's home and healed his mother-in-law (Matthew 8:14-17). Peter even had the experience of walking on water thanks to Jesus (Matthew 14:29). He is in many ways an exemplary disciple, someone worth imitating. He is exactly the opposite of Judas. Peter is what many of us wish we could be.

Apparently, that is also the way Peter sees himself. He is ready to follow Jesus to the death. He can go wherever it is that Jesus is going, no matter how dangerous or distant the place might be.

Today's passage is then the beginning of a great disillusionment. Peter had illusions about his own firmness and fidelity, and Jesus tells him that he will find the truth to be quite different. We also deceive ourselves regarding our own strength and faithfulness, and Peter's case should serve as a warning so that we may remember that we are not so different from Judas. If Judas betrayed Jesus, Peter denied him. Perhaps we will not go as far as betraying the Lord; but might we deny him?

Act: Remembering also your prayer when we studied Judas, pray: "Lord, you know how often I have denied you, how often I have forgotten you, how often I have failed to give witness about you. Sometimes I allowed myself to be led by fear; other times by mere convenience; and there are other times when I don't know what happened. But the fact is that it is so easy to deny you! And that is why I ask for strength and firmness, so that my witness to you may be clear and constant. I pray you, Lord, allow me not to falter. Amen."

Sixth Day: Read John 14:1-6.

See: The events we study today still take place within the context of Jesus' supper with his disciples. He is still preparing them for his departure, and therefore tells them that they should not be troubled, but should know that he is going ahead of them to prepare a place for them in the home of his Father. But his absence will not be permanent, for he will return to take his disciples to the place where he will be.

Now Jesus says something that may surprise us after the previous conversation, when Peter said that he did not know where Jesus was planning to go. Now Jesus, as if he had not noticed Peter's confusion, says, "and you know the way to the place where I am going."

This troubles Thomas. Thomas is famous because in the end, after the resurrection of Jesus, he expressed doubt, and declared that he would not believe unless he were able to put his fingers in the Master's wounds. But we often forget that this is not Thomas's whole story. We already saw that, when the disciples realized that the path that Jesus was following was dangerous, and that returning to Judea might well cost him his life, it was Thomas who told the others that, if Jesus decided to return to Judea and face such great dangers, they should all go with him and share his peril.

Now it is Thomas who expresses what apparently was the confusion of several of them: "Lord we do not know where you are going. How can we know the way?" To which Jesus responds with one of the best-known sayings in the New

Testament: "I am the way, and the truth, and the life. No one comes to the Father, except through me."

Judge: Tomorrow we shall deal again with some of the issues raised here. For today, let us think a bit more about Thomas and his attitude. Thomas teaches us something we often forget: to ask questions. To not understand exactly all that faith requires and to even have doubts, are not reasons for our Lord to abandon or to condemn us. On the contrary, quite often such questions and such doubts lead to important discoveries, and even to a joyful faith, as in the case of Thomas.

Too often in church we think that those who have no questions, or who do not express their doubts, are better Christians that the rest. It is quite useless and even wasteful to continually ask idle, or merely curious, questions. Asking such questions can easily become an excuse for postponing obedience, or for avoiding it altogether.

Yet, it is also true that those who ask no questions will learn little. If we do not ask what it is that God wants of us now, in our present situation, or what is the significance of a particular doctrine, or what a passage in Scripture may be telling us, we will not grow in faith, nor will we give God the opportunity to lead us to that maturity that God wills for every child of God.

Act: Write the following on your notebook: "When I have a doubt or a question about something, I will ask. And when somebody else has a question, I will take it seriously." Now think about what you have just written. In a week, read it again to see if you have done as you proposed.

Seventh Day: Read John 14:7-14.

See: Yesterday we looked at Thomas's question about where Jesus was going and what was the way there, and Jesus' famous response about being the way, the truth, and the life. But that answer does not quite satisfy the disciples. Now that Thomas has set an example, Philip asks: "Lord, show us the Father, and we shall be satisfied." If Jesus is the way, Philip wishes to know where the way leads. This Philip is the disciple from Bethsaida whom the Greeks approached to take them to Jesus, as we saw last week. The Gospel of John says little about him. Since Philip was one of Jesus' earliest disciples, his questioning Jesus in this passage would seem to express a genuine interest in knowing where Jesus is going, in order to be able to follow him.

If Jesus is the way leading to the Father, Philip wants Jesus to show him the Father. To this the Master responds that those who have seen him have seen the Father, for "I am in the Father, and the Father is in me." Believing in Jesus implies believing this, that in him his disciples may see the Father. Besides, they have seen all the deeds that Jesus has done, and these deeds are a sign that Jesus comes from the Father and is a true representation of the Father.

This in turn leads Jesus to promise them that they too will be able to perform deeds such as he has done, and even greater, for the Father will grant them all they ask in his name: "If in my name you ask me for anything, I will do it."

To understand this, it may help to note that in verse 10 Jesus begins referring to "words," and in the end of that verse is speaking about "works," apparently without any sort of transition. The explanation for this is that in the Bible truth is shown in the identity between words and works. When God speaks, what God utters comes into existence. In God, speaking and doing are one and the same thing. When Jesus acts, God speaks through his deeds. This is part of the meaning of the reference to the "name" in verse 13. A "name" is not only a sound, or a way to call someone's attention. The name *is* the person—and for this reason taking the name of God in vain is such a grave sin. To ask for something "in the name of Jesus" does not mean simply pronouncing that name, or ending a prayer with the formula "in the name of Jesus." It means also asking in Jesus himself, in such a way that it is he who asks. And Jesus promises that all the disciples ask in such a fashion will be granted to them.

Judge: This passage, along with the one we studied yesterday, brings a word of promise for the disciples, whom Jesus will leave behind. Here, Jesus promises two things. First, he tells them that though he is leaving, he is not abandoning them; on the contrary, he is going to prepare a place for them. He does not simply leave us behind, as if we were not important. He is taking care of our needs and of our future. He also promises that even while we await the final day, we shall not be left alone. **H.S.**

This passage, as well as others dealing with the same subject, is particularly valuable for us who, like those disciples when what Jesus foretold came to pass, are living in the time between the resurrection and the final consummation. We cannot see him in the flesh, as those disciples did during that supper. As a result, sometimes we feel alone and abandoned. But the truth is exactly the opposite. Rather than being alone and uncared for, we have, right there next to the Father, the Lord who so loved us that he gave up his own life for us. Rather than being alone and friendless, we have a Friend right there at the heavenly throne and the seat of all power.

This is the background for the rest of the passage, where Jesus promises that he will do whatever we ask of the Father in his name. The same power that was manifested when he was with us in the flesh is still present and available to those who follow him today.

Sometimes it is difficult for us to believe this. At other times we read this passage as if it meant that Jesus was giving us a blank check to order whatever we wish. But when we try to cash in the check and what we ask for does not happen, doubt and disillusion ensue. At this point, it is important to remember that the promise refers only to what we ask *in his name*. It is not a blank check. It is a promise that requires that whatever we ask for, be *in his name*.

And, more than a mere formula such as "we pray in the name of Jesus," this means that whatever we ask for must conform to the ways and the goals of Jesus. The name of Jesus is not a magical charm, a Christian sort of "abracadabra," so that by merely repeating it we have the power to do whatever we wish. The name of Jesus is the same as the will of Jesus. To ask "in his name" means to ask according to his will. When our will follows his, there is no doubt that what we ask for will be granted.

The problem is that quite often we ask in what actually amounts to a different name, even if we say "in the name of Jesus." For instance, we call for a miracle so that others may be convinced of our power to perform such miracles. Or we ask for a miracle because that would be most convenient for us, or because it would make us feel good, or because it would prevent difficulties. Certainly, we should ask for whatever we truly wish. But we must also ask that our wishes be truly conformed to the will of God.

Shortly before being betrayed, Jesus himself gave us an example of this by asking the Father that, if at all possible, he be spared the bitter drink of the cross, but asking also, not that his own will be done, but that the Father's will be done. If we pray according to this example, Jesus promises that we will do even greater things than he did!

Act: Pray: "Lord, teach me to pray with faith and in obedience. With faith, knowing that prayer is indeed powerful, that you listen, and that you respond in love. In obedience, so that my desires may be in agreement with your will, and my prayer may be truly in your name. Amen."

For Group Study

Return to yesterday's passage and study it jointly with today's. Encourage the group to speak frankly about things troubling them—about their concerns, both personal and communal. There will be problems mentioned in their families, their employment, and their church. Some will probably mention wider issues of our day, such as the increase in drug abuse, terrorism, the pollution of the environment, international tensions, and growing poverty. Admit, and help the group admit, that all these issues produce anxiety in us. But then insist that, rather than simply being troubled by them, we are to pray about them and do as much as we can about them.

Make a list of all these concerns and invite the group to raise each of them in prayer, always in the name of Jesus. Insist that, when we pray for something, we are also committing to do whatever we can to achieve it. While praying about each of these issues, lead the group in a discussion about what we are called to do about them.

Close the session with a general prayer, presenting your discussion and your resolutions before God.

W E E K

NINE

Michael Welker
⊖ the ψ pg 28 – def.

First Day: Read John 14:15-21.

See: The setting is still the last supper of the Lord with his disciples, just before the betrayal. Jesus continues to tell them about the time when he will no longer be with them. In the passages for today and tomorrow two themes are interwoven. The first is that those who love Jesus will keep his commandments (14:15). This theme will reappear tomorrow in verses 21 and 23-24, as we shall see.

The second theme is the Holy Spirit (14, 16-17, 26). He is called "another Advocate." Jesus, their present advocate, will soon no longer be with them; but the Spirit will take his place. The Spirit is also called "the Spirit of truth." (The word that the NRSV translates as "Advocate" is "Paraclete," and that is why the Spirit is sometimes called "the Paraclete.")

There is a close relationship between Jesus and the Holy Spirit. When the Spirit comes, the world will not know him or see him; but believers will know him. And, precisely because they will have the Spirit, they will also see Jesus, even though the world will no longer be able to see him physically. The Spirit and the Son are not the same; but they are so close, that those who have one have the other. This is similar to the relationship between the Father and the Son: Jesus is not the Father, but those who see him see the Father. Those who have the Spirit see Jesus, and know that Jesus is in the Father. When the disciples are in Jesus, they are also in the Father. And this all leads to the conclusion that those who love Jesus and keep his commandments are themselves loved by Jesus and by the Father.

Judge: There are several important points to be drawn from this passage. The first is the close relationship between Father, Son, and Holy Spirit. This has practical importance, for sometimes we tend to think that there are other ways to know God that are better than Jesus himself. Thus, for instance, some people think that philosophical and rational arguments about God's existence and nature give us a more precise view of God than does Jesus. Others believe that God is best known by looking at the wonders of nature. But the fact is that there is nothing, and no place, where we can come to know God better than in Jesus. Then there are those who think that having the Holy Spirit is somehow better or higher than having Jesus. The fact is that it is impossible to have Jesus without having the Spirit, and that no one can have the Spirit without having Jesus (see 1 Corinthians 12:3).

The second point to be drawn from this passage is that loving Jesus and keeping his commandments go hand in hand. Jesus does not wait until we keep his commandments to love us. He loves us even in our sin. But this does not mean that his commandments are not important. True love for Jesus leads to keeping his commandments.

In the life of the church, as well as in our individual lives, there are two errors that must be avoided. The first is believing that Christianity is a series of rules and commandments. When we think that this is so, we make of those rules the foundation for Christian living, and our preaching is little more than a set of rules, a system of morality. But this is not the Christian message, which is essentially the message of the love of God shown to us in Jesus Christ. It is Jesus Christ, and not a set of rules, that gives new life. Jesus Christ is the center of our faith.

The opposite error lies in thinking that rules and discipline have nothing to do with Christian living. Sometimes we would like to think that it is enough to call ourselves Christian, or to raise our hand in a revival, or to say that we are born again. The fact is that if we are truly Christians—that is, if we truly love Jesus—we will seek to do his will and follow his commandments. To say that we love Jesus, but then to do as we please and not as he says, is sheer hypocrisy.

But there is more. If we truly love Jesus, we will seek to discover his will. We shall not be content with following his commandments in a superficial way, or simply doing what we are told by others that we should do. We shall eagerly seek to discover what his commandments mean for our obedience in each new day and new situation. For instance, there is no doubt that Jesus has commanded us to love our neighbor; but if we really wish to do his will, we must look around us to discover what other people's needs are and how we may serve them.

Act: Write the following on your notebook: "Lord, because I love you, I _____." Now fill in the blank.

Repeat the exercise, filling the blank in a different way. Thus you will have a list of some of the things that your love for Jesus means for you and for your actions.

If possible, try to write some of these sentences in the past tense, and others in the future tense, so they will express something you have done for love of Jesus, and something you propose to do. (For instance: "Lord, because I love you, I went yesterday to visit Jane, who is sick and lonely." Or: "Lord, because I love you, I will continue studying your Word every day.")

Second Day: Read John 14:22-31.

See: Today's passage and yesterday's belong together. In fact, if you read them one after the other you will note that the argument here does not move forward in a straight line, as is the case with the narratives we have studied. It actually moves like a spiral: it makes a point, then another, then another, and then returns to the first point. Although this may seem repetitious, it serves to establish the connection between the various themes in the passage.

We are still at the last supper, and Judas (not the betrayer, but the other disciple, later known as Saint Jude) asks Jesus how it is that he will be able to show himself to the disciples, and not to the rest of the world. The question shows that he understands something of what Jesus is saying, but is puzzled by what he does not understand. If Jesus will no longer be with them physically and visibly so that the world will no longer be able to see him, how are they to see him?

Jesus' answer is that those who love him and keep his commandments will have, not only Jesus, but also the Father and the Holy Spirit, dwelling in them. It is in this way that his followers will see him, even though the world cannot see him. Furthermore, the reason why Jesus has told them all of this is so that when they can no longer see him physically they will not think that he has abandoned them. The Spirit will also confirm to them later on that what they are experiencing is precisely what Jesus told them would occur.

As a result of all this, Jesus leaves his peace to his disciples, but at the same time tells them that this is a different sort of peace. To understand this, it helps to remember that the word "peace" was a common greeting at the time. But that greeting did not mean much, and those offering it seldom thought about what they were saying. (Much as today we say to someone, "How are you?" but do not really expect an answer.) In contrast, when Jesus says "peace" that is exactly what he means and what he gives. Second, the difference between the peace of the world and the peace of Jesus is that the latter is not subject to the vicissitudes of the world.

The passage ends with another announcement of the passion, and an affirmation of the power of Jesus even over evil: ". . . for the ruler of this world is coming. He has no power over me." And yet, so that the world will know his love for the Father and because this is what the Father commands, Jesus will subject himself to the power of death.

This brings us to the end of the long narrative in John about the events of the Lord's last supper with his disciples before the passion.

Judge: Since the passage is about commandments and the need to keep them, consider the following case: Imagine that you buy a toy to give to someone, and upon opening the carton you find that it is not assembled. There are dozens of loose parts. You can try to put it together without consulting the instructions; but if you do so, probably after several tries you will have to confess your failure, and start over following the manufacturer's instructions. The one who made the toy knows how it is supposed to be put together, and how it should function. The instructions that come with it are not just a whim on the part of the manufacturer—a wasteful use of paper and ink. They are a sign that the manufacturer wishes to make sure that the toy will function properly, and produce the satisfaction it was intended to produce.

The same is true of God's commandments. They are our manufacturer's instructions. They are not capricious, but are rather the result of God's love for us, wishing us to be able to live and to function as intended. We can decide to ignore those instructions; but if we do so, in the end we will have to confess our failure—or it will be declared for us in the day of judgment. God's commandments and God's love are two sides of a single coin.

Saint Augustine wrote something that has often been misunderstood. He said: "Love God and do as you please." What do you think about such a statement? Is it a good piece of advice? While thinking about this, remember that the passage we are studying does not say only that we are to keep Jesus' commandments; it says also that he will send the Holy Spirit to remind us of those commandments, to teach us all things, and to help us be obedient. When Jesus says that we shall not be orphaned, this is not only a promise of company; it is also a promise of help and of power. We are not alone in our efforts to obey his commandments. On the contrary, Jesus himself has sent another Advocate, the Holy Spirit, by whose power we are enabled to obey.

Act: Pray: "Thanks, dear God, that now that we cannot see Jesus in the flesh we have the Holy Spirit to remind us of all that Jesus has taught us. I pray that your Spirit will teach me and your church all things, so that we may be able to respond to the needs of today as you wish. I pray in the name of Jesus, and in the power of the Spirit whom he sent. Amen."

Third Day: Read John 15:1-17.

See: This is the well-known passage where Jesus compares himself with a grapevine. One of the main tasks of the person in charge of a vineyard is to prune away the branches that will not bear fruit, and to care for those that will. Here Jesus says that there are branches that bear fruit and others that do not. Those that bear no fruit are to be cut and destroyed, while the rest will receive special attention so that they may bear even more fruit.

Jesus explains the meaning of this allegory, saying that he is the true vine, and that we are branches that can only bear fruit if we are grafted into him.

The text then moves on to explain how we are to be in that vine that is Jesus. In various ways, we are told that being in Jesus means abiding in his love and obeying his commandments. This love and those commandments are so entwined that they cannot be separated. Jesus makes this point twice: "If you keep my commandments, you will abide in my love," and "This is my commandment, that you love one another as I have loved you." The commandment leads to love, and love results in obedience to the commandment.

Finally, the text speaks of a new relationship between Jesus and his followers: "I do not call you servants any longer, ... but I have called you friends." Although here the imagery changes, the point is the same. Instead of speaking of a grapevine and its branches, Jesus refers to the difference between two sorts of relationship. The relationship between Jesus and his disciples, even though he is the Lord, is not like that between a servant or a slave and a master, but rather a relationship of friendship. This is so because the disciples know the designs of their Lord.

The last verse summarizes all of this by once again joining love and obedience: "I am giving you these commandments so that you may love one another."

Judge: Today's passage speaks of the close relationship we are to have with Jesus as true disciples. The image of the grapevine and the branches merits some thought. A branch cannot live by and of itself. If it is cut from the vine, it will wither and die. And it will not suffice for a branch merely to be close to the vine. It has to be grafted into the vine. The vine's sap must flow through the branch, carrying the necessary nutrition from the roots to the branch.

In all circulatory systems, such as the sap in a plant or blood in a body, there is a two-way stream. Blood flows from the heart and the lungs to the members, and then returns to the heart and the lungs. Likewise, in the Christian life there are two directions that are part of a single life. Jesus loved us and gave his life for us. He gives us his love as well as the commandment to love. In response, we are to be obedient to that commandment, abiding in his love and loving one another.

In theory, this sounds quite simple. But Christian life is practice, not just theory. Therefore, we must constantly ask, what does the commandment of love mean for us today? If today I am to abide in the love of Jesus, whom am I to love, and how?

Act: Reflect on the question above. Think of someone you would rather not love. That is precisely the person whom you are called to love. (We do not need to be commanded to love people we like. That comes naturally. It is love for the others that requires a commandment.) Write the name of that person. Now think about "how": what can you do to love that person and act in love for that person? Write down your reflections. Return to these notes in a few days, to see how you are doing.

Fourth Day: Read John 15:18-27.

See: Jesus is still preparing his disciples (and us) for the day when he will no longer be physically present on earth. He begins by warning them that the world will hate them, and that they should not find this surprising, for they are not of the world. Since a servant cannot be more than the master, if their Lord was not spared persecution, neither should his followers expect to be.

On the other hand, there is good reason for people to hate Jesus and his followers, for the very fact that Jesus has come has left them without an excuse. Had Jesus not come and given so many signs of his power and authority, they would have no sin—that is, no sin in this respect. But now those who have rejected him have sinned in that very rejection. It is that sin, and the desire to hide it, that leads the world to persecute Jesus as well as his followers.

This would seem to imply that once Jesus spoke and gave people a chance to believe, they have no other opportunity to believe. But that is not quite the case, for Jesus himself has been telling his disciples that the other Advocate (that is, the Holy Spirit) will give witness to Jesus, and so will the disciples, empowered by the Spirit. That witness, as when Jesus gave it directly, is an opportunity for belief; but it also adds condemnation for those who reject it.

Judge: As we read these words of Jesus, it is quite easy for us to imagine that the conflict between Jesus and "the world" ended when the majority of society—at least of Western society—declared itself Christian. That is true to a degree, for after the fourth century Christians were not persecuted by the Roman Empire, as they had been before. But we must take care, for if we imagine that there is no longer any reason for conflict between Christianity and "the world," we are greatly mistaken. Along these lines, there are two fairly common mistakes.

The first such mistake is to think that there is no longer any conflict or reason for conflict between Christianity and "the world." Were that the case, to be a good Christian it would suffice to be a good, decent, honest, dependable person. This view is fairly common among believers of relatively high social standing, who find it difficult to see much that needs fixing in the present order of society. But the fact is that Christians can never be satisfied with "the world" as long as there are people hungry or in any other sort of need, or as long as there are wars, political and economic deceit, and so forth. Furthermore, there are many places where Christians are still persecuted, with the result that more Christians have died for their faith in the last fifty years than in the first four centuries of persecution.

The other mistake is to think that what the Bible means by "the world" in this negative sense refers particularly to physical creation, or to matter. No. According to the Bible the physical world is God's creation. God acts in it. And God also acts in the world of human relations, of politics, and of economics. To flee "the world" is not to go live in isolation on a deserted island, but to live in the midst of society while not buying into those values and practices that oppose the will of God. Still, there are many Christians, particularly among those belonging to the marginalized segments of society, who think that "the world" is everything that is not the church, and who therefore eschew all social contact with those who are not part of the church.

According to the Bible, the world as a physical reality is God's work. God loves the world. "God so loved the world, that he gave his only Son." If Jesus came into the world, we cannot ignore that world. Yet the world did not receive him, and will not gladly receive his followers. Why? Because the world likes its own order, its own privileges, its own comfort, its own injustice.

Thus, our mission is to love the world, not in order to imitate it or to learn from its corrupt system of privilege and injustice, but so that our own love may be a sign of God's love—and of God's judgment upon those who refuse to love. Sadly, when we do this, the world hates us, just as it hated Jesus because it did not wish to accept him or his teachings.

Act: Pray: "Forgive me, Lord, for the many times I have sought to gain the respect or the affection of the world by acquiescing to its order or profiting from its injustices. And yet, help me continue loving the world; to love it by showing to it your love and your justice. If the world hates me, give me the strength to remain firm. I pray in the name of Jesus, who came into the world, who loved the world, who gave himself for the world, and who was killed by the world. Amen."

Fifth Day: Read John 16:1-4.

See: The warning continues. Its purpose is "to keep you from stumbling"; that is, so that when these things come to pass they will not catch the disciples unawares.

But now the warning becomes dire. Those who will persecute the disciples will not always do this out of evil intent, but with the conviction that they are serving God. We are faced here with the religious dimension of persecution, for the disciples will be expelled from the synagogues, and this will be done in the name of God.

This is the most surprising of all these warnings: the disciples of Jesus will be persecuted in the name of the same God who sent him. This is so astonishing that the Lord tells the disciples about it twice, both at the beginning and at the end of this passage. He does this, once again, so that they will not be surprised and caused to stumble.

Judge: Remember the parents of the blind man who had been healed. They did not dare say he had been cured by Jesus, because they feared being expelled from the synagogue. This was seen as a serious punishment. It was a sign of condemnation both social and religious. Thus, when Jesus tells his disciples—all of them good Jews—that they will be expelled from the synagogues, he is telling them about serious and painful persecution.

Christians today don't have synagogues. But we do have churches. And, sad to say, repeatedly throughout history people have been expelled from churches for no other crime than taking the words and teachings of Jesus quite seriously. Indeed, one of the reasons there are so many Protestant denominations is that we still have not learned to listen to others, to see if what they are saying or doing may be something God wants us to hear and to see. When we find ourselves in disagreement, too often we simply expel or reject those who hold different views; or it is we who leave our former community of faith. In some cases, Christians even curse each other, thinking that in so doing they are serving God.

When we do such things, we are heirs to those ancient synagogues that expelled the very first Christians. Could we not be a little more tolerant? A bit less sure of ourselves? Could we not give more time for new ideas, different ways of doing things, to help us discern whether or not they come from God?

Act: Think of some person with whom you have had an impor-tant disagreement—if the disagreement was about what the church ought to be doing, even better. Approach that person. Ask to have a friendly conversation, in order to try to see what value there may be in that other person's positions. Ask that person to judge what you say and suggest on the basis of the Word of God. Do likewise with whatever that person may be saying.

Sixth Day: Read John 16:5-11.

See: Jesus continues his farewell, and further explains the promise of the Advocate or Comforter. Here Jesus insists that his disciples are not to be saddened by his departure, for it is only after that departure that the Advocate—the Holy Spirit—will come. The role of the Advocate is not limited to the church and to believers, but has to do with the whole world: "when he comes, he will prove the world wrong about sin and righteous-ness and judgment."

This particular verse is difficult to understand, especially since the Greek word that is translated as "prove" means much more than that. For us, to "prove" means to convince, to leave no room for doubt. Here, it does mean that; but it also means more. It also means to show, as a lawyer does in the presence of a court, and therefore it has connotations of judgment and con-demnation. This should help us understand verses 9-11:

• The Advocate proves the sin of the world in not believing Jesus (verse 9).

• The Advocate manifests righteousness (which also means justice) because he stands for Jesus, who is God's righteousness (verse 10).

• The Advocate shows or proves the judgment of God, because the Evil One has already been judged and found guilty, and the Advocate will make this manifest (verse 11).

Judge: In many of our churches we say that we "rejoice in the Spirit." This has good biblical foundation, for in this passage Jesus tells us that, rather than being saddened because he is not with us, we should rejoice at having the Advocate with us.

On the other hand, however, too often when we in the church rejoice in the presence of the Spirit, we forget that the Spirit also has a role in the world around us. The Spirit confirms the sin of those who refuse to believe. The Spirit confirms the justice or righteousness of God revealed in Jesus Christ. And the Spirit is a sign that the judgment of God, by which evil is condemned, is already a reality.

Perhaps this is the reason why the world around us so often seems to look down on those Christians who insist that they have the Spirit of God—because it secretly realizes that our joy in the Spirit is also proof of its own sin, of its own refusal to believe. And the counterpart of this is also true: perhaps, when the surrounding society does not criticize Christians, and lets us be, this is because we limit the function of the Spirit to our own community, and do not see how the presence of the Spirit is also a word of judgment on the world.

Act: Pray, asking the Holy Spirit to give and increase in you the joy of the Spirit's presence, even while we all await the day of the final consummation. Ask the Spirit to give you words and actions that may be a faithful witness before the world.

Write a prayer asking for these things. Repeat it, while you reflect on what you are asking. If there are others in your church or community who are following this series of studies at the same time as you, share with some of them the prayer you have written.

Seventh Day: Read John 16:12-24.

See: Jesus continues preparing his disciples for his passion and death. He even adds that there are other things he could tell them, but that "you cannot bear them now." Given the context, these things that the disciples cannot bear are the actual passion, death, and resurrection of their Master. Perhaps Jesus is referring specifically to the manner in which the authorities will plot to destroy him. Later, when all these things have passed, the Spirit will help the disciples understand their significance.

The Master tells them that soon they will see him no more,

[handwritten margin notes: reflect on this... what could it be?]

and that then they will see him again. The disciples don't understand this. Then Jesus tells them that they will undergo a time of pain and lamentation, but that after this their sadness will turn into joy.

As an explanation, Jesus tells them of a woman in childbirth. The pains of childbirth are great and quite real. They do not disappear simply because she knows that she is about to have a child. Yet once the child is born, the joy is such that the pain and the anguish of birth are left behind. Then there is only room for joy because this new child has come into the world. Likewise, Jesus tells his disciples, a time of pain and sadness now approaches; but Jesus will see them again. When he returns, no one will be able to take away from his disciples the joy of his presence.

Meanwhile, although Jesus will not be there to explain to them what has happened, nor its meaning, the Holy Spirit—the Spirit of Truth—will be with them to lead them to "all truth." Here we see a common thread throughout the Gospel of John: the Spirit is not a reality independent of Jesus, as if the Spirit's teachings were different or above those of Jesus. On the contrary, "He will glorify me, for he will take what is mine and declare it to you."

Judge: When speaking these words, Jesus was preparing his disciples for his absence between the crucifixion and the resurrection. The illustration of the woman in childbirth, and the ensuing great joy, refer primarily to the disciples' pain upon seeing their Lord accused, tried, condemned, and crucified, and then their joy upon seeing him arisen after the third day. The disciples would undergo a painful period between the time of the arrest of Jesus and the time of his resurrection.

But the text also refers to another situation which, although less dramatic, is no less real. After his resurrection, the Lord did not remain physically with his disciples. We too, live "between the times"—between the time of his ascension and the time of his return in glory. We live in the time of the physical absence of

Jesus, and this causes pain and perplexity. This is precisely the reason why the Gospel of John underscores the time of the absence of Jesus between the crucifixion and the resurrection—and also the reason why it stresses the presence of the Holy Spirit among the disciples as they live "between the times."

When this Gospel was written, the church was already living in circumstances similar to ours: between the time of the ascension and the time of the Kingdom. In such circumstances, it was important to remember that already at an earlier time the first disciples had undergone a similar time of physical absence—a time even more difficult than ours, for they had not yet seen the resurrection of their Lord.

The promise of the Spirit is precisely for a time such as ours, for a time "between the times." While the Lord is not physically present among us, the Holy Spirit accompanies us and leads us to "all truth." At this point, let us not forget verses 12-15: the truth to which the Spirit leads is none other than Jesus Christ himself. In John 14:6, Jesus declares that he is the truth. It is not a matter of Jesus conveying a certain level of truth, and the Spirit conveying a higher level. The Spirit leads to Jesus, not to something above or beyond Jesus. The Spirit is like a light shining on Jesus, so that we may better perceive him, better love him, and better serve him. The Spirit is not a higher revelation for some Christians who are supposedly more "spiritual" than the rest, and who no longer need the Jesus who came in the flesh.

We who live "between the times" are led by the Spirit to be faithful and obedient in our time, but the Spirit always does this by leading us to Jesus. Relating this to our study of John 15, one could say that the Spirit joins us to Jesus so that we may be branches who are firmly grafted into the true vine.

Act: Do you know people who claim that the Spirit reveals to them truths beyond those revealed in Jesus? This may be someone in your own church, or perhaps from another church or denomination. How would you try to correct that person, always in a spirit of love? Write down what you would say.

For Group Study

This session may be a good opportunity to deal with some misunderstandings about "spirituality" that are quite widespread. Some people think that the "spiritual" is that which is not material or physical. This is the reason that some people think that, since Jesus came in physical flesh, his teachings cannot reach the level of the Spirit. But there are two errors in such a view.

First, such people seem to forget that it is impossible to know Jesus and to accept him as Lord and Savior, except by the work of the Spirit. Therefore, anybody who is truly a Christian has the Holy Spirit.

Second, it is not true that the material and the spiritual stand in contrast to each other. In the Bible, "spiritual" refers to anyone who listens to God and obeys God. The opposite of "spiritual" is "carnal," which refers to everything that disobeys God—not only the body, but also the mind.

Explain this to the group. Ask them to make a list of sins that are committed primarily with the mind or with the soul—for instance, greed, pride, hatred—and another list of spiritual things that are done with the body—for instance, feeding the hungry or praying out loud.

W E E K

TEN

First Day: Read John 16:25-33.

See: Finally the disciples begin to understand what Jesus is telling them. In verse 29: "Yes, now you are speaking plainly, not in any figure of speech!"

Jesus responds that, although they finally believe, they should have no illusions about the future. Just as he had told Peter that he would deny him three times, he now tells all the disciples that they will be scattered and will leave him alone—although he also says that he will not be truly alone because the Father is with him.

Note that in verses 26 and 27 Jesus rejects a common opinion about his relationship with the Father. According to that opinion, the Father is a just God who requires punishment for sin, whereas it is the Son who intercedes for us and convinces the Father to be merciful. This is not what the Bible says about God. Jesus says it quite clearly: "I do not say to you that I will ask the Father on your behalf; for the Father himself loves you."

At the end of today's passage, Jesus gives the reason why he has said these things to the disciples: so that they may have peace. Note that he has told them that he not only will suffer, die, and return, but also that they will forsake him. And he has told them this so that they may have peace? When they decide to return after being scattered and forsaking him, they will understand that even though Jesus foresaw their actions, he still loved them.

Finally, the passage ends with the well-known words: "In the world you face persecution. But take courage; I have conquered the world!"

Judge: These last words of the passage have been a source of courage and hope for Christians throughout the ages. What is this "world" where, according to Jesus, we shall face persecution? Here the "world" is not just the physical creation—what in geography classes we call "the world." Rather it is creation and society itself in rebellion against God. The world is that society where the stronger have more rights, where those who command are most worthy, where the purpose of life is "to get ahead"—even at the expense of others. That was the world that Jesus faced in Roman times, and it is the world we face today.

In such a world, believers in Jesus Christ will face difficulties and even persecution. They will not fit, because they insist not on being served, but on serving; not on receiving, but on giving. In this world where all seek their own gain, the disciples of the Master who gave his life for others will not seek gain for themselves, but the good of others. Thus, their very presence and witness will be a challenge to the world, which will therefore hate them.

This world is powerful and apparently all engulfing; but Jesus' followers are to take courage, for their Lord has already conquered the world. How? In his very death and resurrection. As John has already begun to tell us, and will further clarify, the death of Jesus was brought about by a coalition of Judean and Roman leaders, who decided that he must be destroyed. They called to their cause their most powerful ally: Death. But even death was not enough to defeat Jesus. He has conquered death and the world. That is why he can say: "Take courage; I have conquered the world!"

Act: What are the powers of the world that you most fear? List them in your notebook. Some examples might be: The opinion of the "important" people around you; the authority of your superiors and supervisors in your job; the possibility of poverty; ill health. How do you respond to these fears? Do you believe that your responses are those of someone who trusts in the Lord who has conquered the world? Write down your reflections.

Second Day: Read John 17:1-3.

See: Several times in the Gospel of John we have encountered the phrase "the hour" or "my hour." Usually this refers to the time of the arrest, trial, and crucifixion of Jesus. Now, after several chapters in which John tells us how Jesus prepared his disciples for this time, the "hour" has arrived. After speaking to his disciples, Jesus addresses the Father in prayer.

This prayer, which encompasses all of chapter 17, is often called the Priestly Prayer of Jesus because in it Jesus intercedes for his disciples and for those who will follow later. Whereas in the previous chapters Jesus told his disciples what he expected of them in the future, now he tells the Father.

The prayer begins with a petition to the Father, that Jesus be glorified. This may seem strange, for if one of us were to pray saying "Father, glorify me," that would be a very prideful and even foolish request. But in this case we must remember two points.

Given the unity between Jesus and the Father of which John has spoken repeatedly, the glory of the Son is also the glory of the Father. Thus in glorifying Jesus the Father glorifies himself. Besides, given that close union and the eternal origin of the Son next to the Father (remember the very first verses of John), when Jesus asks to be glorified he is not asking for something that does not already belong to him.

The second and most important point is that the glorification Jesus requests is very different from what we often understand by glorification. Jesus is facing the cross, and he asks the Father that in that hour he may be glorified. This glorification is not a matter of wearing a crown, of receiving praise, or of being clothed in splendor. It is a matter of being obedient at the very moment of the cross. Thus, just as Jesus rejects the world's priorities—where the most powerful and most abusive are also the most important—he also takes for himself a different understanding of "glory," which consists in serving, in giving himself up, in being obedient.

Judge: Once we understand glory in this way there is nothing wrong in praying: "Father, glorify me so that I may also glorify you." In thus praying, what we are asking is not to be praised, admired, or obeyed, but rather that God's will may be done in us—that we may better serve others and may be able to do this in such a way that God will receive the honor and the praise. Whether or not the result is that we are praised, admired, or followed, is to be left in the hands of God. This is not to be the purpose of our actions.

What do you think would happen if there were in the world many more believers truly ready to have their Lord glorified in them, even at the expense of their comfort, prestige, power, or wealth?

Act: Pray: "Lord, I dare ask you to glorify me—yet not as the world understands glory, but rather as your Son manifested it in his life and his death. Give me the faith and the power to face whatever you will in such a way that you may be glorified. I pray in the name of Jesus, who glorified you in his suffering. Amen."

Third Day: Read John 17:4-11.

See: The Priestly Prayer of Jesus continues. Note that in verse 5 Jesus says what we saw yesterday, that in asking the Father to glorify him he is merely asking for what was his from the beginning.

Now the focus of attention shifts to the disciples for whom Jesus prays. He specifies that he is not praying for the world at large, but for the disciples. What he asks for them is that they may be guarded and protected. Note, however, the purpose for which Jesus asks that his disciples be guarded: "So that they may be one, as we are one." On the basis of what we hear most commonly about what Jesus desires for us, we would expect him to ask the Father to guard us so that we may be saved, or so that we may obey his commandments, or so that we may worship God. All of this is important; but what Jesus asks above all is that his followers may be one. And that unity must be similar to the relationship between the Father and the Son.

Judge: If a group of people in your church were asked to state what they believe to be Jesus' most urgent desire for his disciples, what do you think they will answer? Possibly some will say that Jesus wants us to believe; others will say that he wants us to be faithful; others will say that he wants us to witness to the world. Clearly, all of these are good things, and there is no doubt that Jesus wants them for us.

The first thing that Jesus asks the Father for us is that we may be one. Christian unity is not a secondary matter. It is not something that we should seek only after we have solved all other problems. It is the very first thing that Jesus asks for his followers. Further on, we shall see that this is related to our witness before the world. But for the time being, it is important that we center our attention on unity as Jesus' desire for us.

In truth, most of us have paid scant attention to this matter of unity. We certainly believe that Christians should not fight among themselves; but that is not quite the same as insisting that unity is one of the central traits of Christian discipleship.

Act: Think about some of the issues, problems, and disagreements that threaten unity in your congregation. What can you do to strengthen the bond of union in your congregation?

Now think about the various churches in your community. What is it that keeps them apart? Are they matters so serious that they warrant division among believers? Could it be that many of our divisions persist simply because we do not realize how important unity is for Christian living?

Think about what you and other members of your church can do to develop closer bonds with other churches in your neighborhood. Write down your reflections and share them with others in your congregation. Jointly, take some steps to approach those other churches.

Fourth Day: Read John 17:12-17.

See: Jesus is still praying for his disciples. He speaks as if he were no longer in the world, for he knows that he goes to the

Father. His disciples will be left behind, and it is for them that he prays. Now that he will no longer be with them, he asks the Father to guard them, as he guarded them while he was among them.

He does not ask that they be taken out of the world. He does not ask the Father to make a special world for them, nor that they be carried away to a spiritual realm. He knows that his disciples are to continue living in the world. Therefore he asks the Father that, even while remaining in the world, they be kept from evil. By evil, Jesus doesn't simply mean bad things that might happen to them. Jesus asks the Father that his followers be kept from the power of the Evil One, of that evil that is so deeply rooted in the world and in the midst of which the disciples will have to live.

Finally, Jesus asks the Father that the disciples be sanctified in the truth, which is none other than the Word of God.

Judge: The place of Christians in the world requires serious reflection. It is not the will of Jesus that we live in a different world where we may be kept pure. However, quite often that is precisely what we expect the church to be. We tell ourselves that since there is so much evil in the world, the church must be a substitute for the world from which we wish to distance ourselves. When this happens, the church becomes a sort of private club for holy people, building around itself spiritual and psychological walls that are very similar to the walls surrounding the exclusive clubs of high society. That walled church then becomes a refuge where we can live without the uncertainties and temptations of the world. The problem is that such a walled church cannot witness to Jesus in the world. If we do not rub shoulders with people in the world, how are we to witness to them?

On the other hand, this does not mean that when we decide to follow Jesus we should simply continue living as we did in "the world." There is a difference in Christian life; but the difference is not in that we build walls around ourselves, but rather that we begin to judge matters by different standards. Thus, while in the world the greatest is the one who has the most power, among Christians it is the one who serves most. While the glory of the world is in prestige, wealth, and power, the glory of Christians is in obedience, dedication, and service.

This is why Jesus does not ask the Father to take us away from the world, but to keep us from it—to keep us from those mistaken judgments and from that pride and disobedience that are the essence of the world.

Act: Make a list of people with whom you relate outside of the community of faith—for instance, in your job, in your business, in your studies, in your pastimes. Ask yourself what you can do in each of these cases to keep the bonds of those relationships, but to do so in such a way that you witness to the Lord Jesus and to a set of values and principles different from those of the world. Write down your answers. If possible, share them with other believers. But in any case, act on them.

Fifth Day: Read John 17:18-23.

See: We are still in the Priestly Prayer of Jesus for his disciples. There are two important elements in this passage. First, it is here that we learn that throughout this prayer Jesus is not praying only for his immediate disciples, but also for all who would follow later—that is, for us.

The second point to notice is the purpose of the unity that Jesus wills his disciples to have. We are to have this unity, not just so we may care for each other and may feel good in the company of our brothers and sisters—important as that is. The purpose of the unity of believers is their witness to the world, which will be more effective if it is a unified witness. Note that this is so important, that the same idea appears both in verse 21 and in verse 23. Jesus wants us to be one, not so that the church may be bigger, but so that the world may believe—which in turn means that, insofar as the world does not believe because we are divided and fight with each other, we are responsible for that unbelief.

Judge: Do you think that Christians in your community give signs of a unity such that it is a positive witness to Jesus Christ? Think first in terms of your local congregation. Is there among your members such unity that people who see them and experience the way they relate among themselves will be inclined to believe on the basis of that unity and the love behind it? Or are there jealousies, cliques, and ill feelings that may be an obstacle on other people's path to faith?

Now think about your neighborhood or your town. How many Christian churches are there in your town or community? How do they relate among themselves? Do they compete with each other? Do they try to lure away each other's members? Do they collaborate in some project or projects? When people in your town or community see these churches, do they see even a glimpse of that unity that Jesus prayed we should have and does that glimpse move them to faith?

Finally, think in denominational terms. Is your denomination committed to Christian unity? How is it showing that commitment? Or does it think that its own particular points of doctrine or of practice are so important that other Christians who have different doctrines and practices are not true believers?

Note also that quite often our divisions have no other reason for existing than inertia. We simply are not sufficiently interested in seeking and manifesting unity. What do you think Jesus would say about these divisions that continue simply because they began years ago, and nobody seems interested in mending the fences?

Act: Resolve to discuss these issues with at least three people: another member of your local congregation, a member of another church in your town or neighborhood, and some denominational leader. Explore with each of them what Christians today can do so that the world may see us more united, and thus come to belief.

Pray: "Father, we ask that we may all be one, as you and the Son are one, so that the world may believe that you did send him. Perfect us in love and in unity, so that the world may know that you have loved us as you love your Son. In his name we pray as he prayed. Amen."

Sixth Day: Read John 17:24-26.

See: These verses conclude the Priestly Prayer of Jesus, which includes all of chapter 17. Here, one of the themes is that the Son reveals the Father, so that those who follow Jesus know the Father. The other main theme is Jesus' request that his disciples may be with him where he is going—that is, in heaven.

It is here, at the very end of the prayer, that Jesus addresses what many people think is the very heart of the gospel: that we are to live eternally with him. This is certainly part of the message of the gospel, which could hardly be called "good news" without such a promise. But, as we have seen throughout this entire prayer, what Jesus wishes to accomplish with us goes much further. Jesus wishes us to keep his commandments and to love him. Jesus wills us to be one, and also wills us to share in his glory. All of this is part of his prayer for us. And it is all entwined in such a way that without one of these elements it is difficult to wish or to hope for the rest.

Judge: Now that we are completing our study of the Priestly Prayer of Jesus for his disciples—those of his day as well as us—we see that the gospel is much more than the promise of eternal life for those who believe in Jesus. The gospel is also an invitation to accept God's love and to respond in love. It is an invitation to keep the commandments of God, not out of obligation or out of fear, but out of love and faithfulness. The gospel is also a call to such unity and love that, upon seeing us, the world will believe.

Unfortunately, these other facets of the gospel are preached and taught much less frequently than the promise of life eternal. Sometimes they seem like footnotes to a gospel that is only a message of salvation. The danger then is that we may end up with a partial gospel, which is not the full or true gospel of Jesus Christ. And, because our gospel is incomplete, we do not practice the love, faithfulness, and unity that are part of what God desires for us and promises to give us.

Act: Make a list of the various dimensions of the gospel mentioned above, such as personal salvation, love of God, obedience to the commandments of God, love and unity among believers, and so on. Add other aspects of Christian life that seem important to you—for instance, the quest for social justice, responsibility toward the environment, stewardship. Write down the entire list in your notebook.

Now, with that list in mind, talk with your pastor and with other leaders of your congregation to see how you can help these various dimensions of the gospel find better expression in your life, as well as in the life of your congregation. Offer to do whatever you can to achieve this.

Seventh Day: Read John 18:1-11.

See: This story is well known, though sometimes we forget the details. Jesus had gone with his disciples (except Judas) to a secluded place where they had met on other occasions. This was in a garden next to the valley of Kidron. At the bottom of this valley there was a creek that ran precipitously from Jerusalem toward the Dead Sea. During the high times of the monarchy, the kings had their gardens in this valley. The stream of Kidron had always been considered the city limits of Jerusalem. When John tells us that Jesus and his disciples went across the valley of Kidron he means that they left the city of Jerusalem. This is important because those who were coming to arrest Jesus wanted to do this in a secluded place where they would not risk a riot. One of the crimes the Romans punished most severely was rioting. Remember that those who were conspiring to kill Jesus were afraid that if his fame grew the Romans would intervene and Judea would lose some of the scant freedoms it still enjoyed. For that reason, the last thing they wanted was to create a riot by arresting Jesus. This helps us understand what it was that Judas did. He did not accuse Jesus or tell his enemies of his teachings, for these were well known. His betrayal consisted in leading those who wished to arrest him to a place where he would be found alone with his disciples.

Jesus and his disciples were in the garden when they came to arrest him. Since the text says that they came with lanterns and torches, it does not seem that the soldiers, the police, and others who came to arrest him came in secret. The arrest would be made public after the fact, when rioting would be less likely. On the other hand, the fact that they came armed indicates that even though they did not think that they had to arrest Jesus by stealth, they feared there might be some resistance.

Although Jesus knows that he is the one they seek, he still asks them for whom they are looking. The power of his presence is such that those who come to arrest him step back and fall to the ground. Jesus finally turns himself in while also asking those who came to arrest him to let his disciples go. If he is the only one they seek, they have no reason to arrest the others.

Peter's reaction is well known. He drew his sword and cut off the ear of one of the servants of the high priest. Since further on we will learn that it was the high priest who had suggested killing Jesus, and probably the disciples knew or suspected this, it is not surprising that Peter would vent his ire on one of the servants of the high priest. The Gospel of John is the only one that tells us his name was Malchus. We are not told whether Malchus was an important person or simply someone who happened to be closest to Peter.

Jesus then tells Peter to sheathe his sword and not resist the lot that Jesus must face: "Am I not to drink the cup the Father has given me?"

Judge: Perhaps the best way to reflect on the significance of this narrative for our own lives is to reflect on two of its characters.

First, there is Judas. Some have suggested that he was in fact a patriot who wished to see Jesus restore the kingdom of Israel, and betrayed him hoping to force his hand into performing a great miracle or declaring war on the Romans. The Bible says nothing about this. It simply states that Judas betrayed Jesus for some silver coins. Without going into speculations, it is clear that Judas betrayed Jesus because he did not share his Master's vision. Whether it was for patriotic motives or for money, the fact is that Judas placed other interests above the teachings of Jesus, and this led him to betray the Master.

We may find it distasteful to compare ourselves with Judas, but the truth is that quite often we risk being like him. We do this when we place other interests above obedience to Jesus and above love for God and neighbor. Although perhaps not openly, we betray Jesus when we make decisions primarily on the basis of money or other benefits to be received, rather than on the basis of love and service to which Jesus calls us. We must confess that such an attitude is quite common in our day. When we allow ourselves to be led away by it, we are approaching the stance of Judas.

It may help to remember that Judas did not go with the others to the meeting across the Kidron. It would seem that one of the ways the values of the gospel begin to be forgotten or postponed and supplanted by the values of the surrounding society is when we begin to draw apart from the company of believers, from common study and worship. When studying and praying together, we confirm each other in the values of the gospel. When we then come to a moment when a decision is required, we are better prepared to make the correct choice. For instance, if we are offered an opportunity that would bring us great profit, but at the cost of other values and principles, we would be much better prepared to resist temptation if we were part of a community that does not think that money is everything—as is so commonly thought in today's society.

The other character that merits some reflection is Peter. His attitude is very different from that of Judas. He is a convinced follower of Jesus. By drawing his sword, he risks being arrested. In that sense his attitude is admirable; but even though it springs from love of the Master, it opposes the will of that very Master. Although he sought to defend Jesus, in fact he was undermining his ministry. Peter was ready to defend Jesus; but that very defense was, in a way, a betrayal of Jesus. The Master showed a power much greater than that of any soldier or Temple police by giving himself up voluntarily, after first showing them that he had the power to resist if he so wished.

By drawing his sword and wounding Malchus, Peter lowers himself to the same level of the soldiers. If it were up to Peter, the whole issue would have been resolved by an armed fight to see who was the most powerful. But this would not solve anything, because if the soldiers won, Jesus would still be arrested and he would have lost the power of his voluntary surrender. If, on the other hand, the disciples won, his entire ministry would be undone, and he would be no more than one of the many rebel leaders that abounded in the countryside.

Are there times when Christians act like Peter? When we go forth in defense of the faith and of Jesus, are we not telling the world that our faith—and Jesus himself—need to be defended? Sometimes, we do this believing we are giving a strong witness, when in fact our witness is being weakened. Even though it seems to be an act of faith, Peter's action shows a lack of faith. Don't we do the same when we act as if Christian truth depended on us, or when we attack the enemies of Christ with such fierce anger that what actually shows is our own insecurity?

Act: Make a list of things you can do to strengthen your commitment to Jesus and to the values of the gospel. Pray, committing yourself to do these things, and ask for help in fulfilling your commitment. If possible, share your thoughts and decisions with others.

For Group Study

Ask the group if they remember when it was that Judas departed from Jesus and the other disciples. (For the answer, look at John 13:30.) Now review with the group some of the things that Judas did not hear, precisely because he was no longer with the other disciples. Suggest that, although Judas had already decided to betray Jesus, his absence from all those conversations must have made his betrayal much easier.

Invite the group to make a list of things we can do to foster our faithfulness, so that we may not betray Jesus.

W E E K
ELEVEN

First Day: Read John 18:12-14.

See: We finally come to the arrest of Jesus and the first steps that will lead to his trial and crucifixion. It is important to note who participated in his arrest. In the passage we studied yesterday, we were told that among those who came to arrest him there was "a detachment of soldiers." Exactly who these soldiers were is not clear in that passage. Although it was only the Romans who had actual soldiers in Judea, the Temple police were sometimes called "soldiers." In today's passage, however, the word translated as "their officer" is a word reserved for a certain Roman military rank. Therefore, the soldiers are apparently Romans—a fact further attested by the additional mention of "the Jewish police" as a separate group.

Thus, it would appear that, although at first it was the Judean religious leaders who decided to destroy Jesus, now they have somehow managed to enroll also the Roman military authorities. This would not have been very difficult, for all that was needed was to tell the Romans that there was a teacher or preacher claiming that he was the King of the Jews. Since claiming such a title would be considered a seditious act against Roman power, the Judean leaders would thus show that they were quite in favor of that power, and at the same time gain the support of Roman authorities for the arrest and trial of Jesus.

The "Jewish police" are probably the Temple guard, whose role was to keep order, particularly in the Temple, but also in any other situation in which crowds had to be controlled, potential riots needed to be suppressed, and so on.

Those who arrest Jesus take him to the house of Annas, the

father-in-law of Caiaphas. Remember that Caiaphas was the one who, upon learning of the resurrection of Lazarus, first mentioned the need to suppress Jesus in order to save the nation (see 11:49-50).

Judge: Upon hearing of this teacher who performed miracles and who drew large numbers of followers, Caiaphas deemed it necessary to destroy Jesus because of his fear that the Romans would intervene and suppress what little freedom and measure of autonomy the Jewish nation still had. In other words, Caiaphas placed his nationalistic interests above truth and even against the very principles on which the Jewish nation was founded, for this was a people supposed to serve the Lord in justice and righteousness.

Similar things happen today. When faced by problems of international injustice, many of us think that our first loyalty must be to our own nation, tribe, or group. But Christians should know that our first loyalty is to the God of all nations. If at any point our patriotism conflicts with our faith, which of the two will prove more important for us?

What is particularly tragic is that sometimes—as in the case of Caiaphas—the view of the "nation" that we decide to protect is a contradiction of the founding principles of the nation itself. Caiaphas's nation was founded on the principle of service to God—a God of justice and equity—yet in defending that nation, Caiaphas is willing to set aside the very law of God. If today we are part of a nation founded on the principle of the equality of humankind and on the right of all people to the pursuit of happiness, what should we do or say when people elsewhere claim their own dignity and equality, and this seems to clash with our national interests?

Act: Look at your own congregation. Does it represent a particular segment of society? A particular culture, race, class? What does your church do to show that the gospel is above all such distinctions? Write down your reflections. Share them with others.

Now, review in your mind the main international headlines of the last few days. Is your country acting according to its own founding principles? If not, begin by at least expressing your disapproval. Write your representatives in Congress, write to your local newspaper. Make your voice heard.

Second Day: Read John 18:15-24.

See: Today we are studying two events that are entwined in the narrative. One is Peter's denial—that is, his first denial. The other is the trial or interrogation of Jesus by the high priest.

The first of Peter's denials takes place just inside the courtyard of the high priest Annas. John tells us that Peter and another disciple, whose name is not given, were following Jesus, apparently to see what happened. When they saw that Jesus was taken to the house of Annas, this other disciple—who was known in that house—went into the courtyard and then made arrangements so that Peter also could come in. It was as Peter was entering the courtyard that the woman who guarded the gate asked Peter if he was "also one of this man's disciples." (Note that the word "also" might imply that the woman knew that the other man was a disciple of Jesus. If so, the question was not necessarily hostile, as we often think.) Peter denied that he was one of the disciples of Jesus, went into the courtyard, and stood there, warming himself by the fire together with the police—presumably the Temple police—and the slaves—apparently, Annas's slaves. The Gospel narrative leaves him there as it turns its attention back to Jesus and to his dialogue with Annas.

The Gospel of John calls this man "the high priest" in verse 19. But verse 24 tells us that the one who questioned Jesus was Annas. The person who in fact occupied that position at the time was his son-in-law Caiaphas. What is happening here is that it was customary to keep giving the title of "high priest" to any who had occupied that position earlier—much as today we refer to "President Carter," when in fact he is no longer president. When John tells us that the one who questioned Jesus was "the high priest," he is referring to Annas, and not strictly to the one who currently occupied that position. This is the reason why Annas sends Jesus to Caiaphas after questioning him.

The Gospel of John says little about the contents of this interrogation at the house of Annas. The reason for this is probably to show that the interrogation itself is little more than a formality. Annas, Caiaphas, and the other religious leaders had long decided that Jesus must die. But Jewish authorities did not have the right to impose the death penalty; therefore, it was necessary for them to make a case before the Romans. And this case must be about a breech of Roman, not Jewish law. They must accuse Jesus of having proclaimed himself "King of the Jews," and therefore fostering sedition among Rome's Jewish subjects—a crime which would certainly carry the death penalty. This is why Jesus refuses to answer. Annas is not seeking the truth, which he could well have learned by asking others, as Jesus tells him. What he is after is having Jesus say something that would serve as a basis for accusing him before the Romans.

When the policeman—apparently in exasperation—strikes Jesus, this makes it all the clearer that right and reason are on the side of Jesus, who very appropriately asks the man to show him what evil he has done. If Jesus has done no wrong, then it is the policeman himself who is wrong.

Eventually, Annas sends Jesus to his son-in-law, Caiaphas, because he has apparently run out of options about what to do with him.

Judge: Annas questions Jesus, not to find the truth, but rather for his own purposes and agenda. This strikes us as an extreme case of hypocrisy and injustice. But the truth is that we ourselves often act in similar ways—although perhaps not to the same degree.

I remember well the first few years of my residence in the United States, and then in Puerto Rico. At that time, emotions ran high, both for and against Castro's policies in Cuba. Quite often, when people learned that I was Cuban, they would ask me about Cuba and what was happening there. I soon discovered, however, that quite often people who asked such questions were not really seeking to learn something about Cuba. They had already made up their minds on the matter. When they asked my opinion, what they were really asking was who I was, and where I stood. If I tried to give a balanced and nuanced response, the result was simply that no one liked what I said, rather than coming to their own more balanced or nuanced position.

We often do the same in the life of the church. We ask someone a question, not really to learn about the subject of the question, but rather to classify the other person—to decide whether he or she is "liberal," "fundamentalist," "charismatic," "reactionary," "moderate," or whatever other name or label concerns us at the time.

Sadly, when conversation descends to that level we dehumanize the other. We do not really listen to them, and we have long decided that they have nothing to teach us. We already know all the labels. What remains is to find out which label we shall tag on this particular person. The result of such dehumanization is that we find ourselves unable to resolve differences, and that we often ride roughshod over the other. Would it not be much better to listen to the other, to establish a real dialogue, and perhaps even learn something from each other?

Act: Write in your notebook a list of whatever terms you have heard in your church or among your fellow believers to classify other Christians—terms such as "fundamentalist," "liberal," "revolutionary," "conservative," "charismatic." Now cross them out one at a time. As you cross each of them out, ask God to help you see beyond such labels. If you can think of someone who could wear the label you are crossing out, try to remember something about that person that has nothing to do with the label itself—her profession, his pain at having lost a loved one, her service to the church, and so on.

Third Day: Read John 18:25-27.

See: Verse 25 picks up the story of Peter's denial where it was left yesterday in verse 18, after his first denial. The passage simply tells of the other two denials, and finally of the crowing of the cock.

Peter's denial takes place in three stages. First, he denies Jesus
in order to be able to remain in the courtyard near him. When
the woman asks him whether he is one of the disciples of Jesus,
if Peter responds that he is indeed one of them, then he will
probably not be let in, or will be expelled by the slaves and the
police in the courtyard. One could then argue that Peter denies
Jesus this first time in order to remain near, to be able to see
what is happening to his Master. By then all the other disciples
had apparently scattered, and only Peter and the unnamed disciple who helped him enter the courtyard had followed Jesus—
though from afar—to see what happened to him. Peter seems to
be more loyal than the rest. And perhaps, as a result of that very
loyalty, he denies Jesus in order to be allowed to remain in the
courtyard.

The second denial takes place under different circumstances.
Jesus has already been questioned by Annas and sent over to
Caiaphas bound. Peter is still in the courtyard, warming himself
by the fire. Quite likely he remains there because he has no idea
where else to go. After all, the warmth of the fire is the only con-
solation he has in this sad evening. Then someone asks him if he
is one of Jesus' disciples. Peter now denies his Master a second
time—no longer to see what happens to the Master, but simply
to remain by the fire unmolested.

The third denial takes place under more difficult circumstances. Now it is one of Malchus's relatives who asks him if he
is one of the disciples of Jesus. He even says that he thinks he
saw Peter at the garden when Jesus was arrested. Although the
man does not say so, his question is almost an accusation that he
suspects that it was Peter who attacked his relative. In any case,
it would have sounded to Peter like such an accusation, whose
consequences could be serious. For a third time, now in order to
save himself, Peter denies Jesus.

With dramatic brevity, John brings the story to an end: "at that
moment the cock crowed."

Judge: All of this should serve to remind us that it is possible to
deny Jesus at several different levels and for different reasons.
Sometimes the very first denials seem to be justified. Peter
denies so that he can stay in the courtyard, close to his Master.

Then he moves a bit further, and denies his Lord for his own convenience. Finally, he denies him because the situation has gotten out of hand, and he fears for himself.

Sometimes we convince ourselves that, were we to find ourselves in a really dramatic situation demanding heroic obedience, like the early martyrs, we would certainly give firm and valiant witness to our faith. We tell ourselves that in such circumstances we would be as firm as a rock—just as Peter, whom Jesus had named "Rock," thought he would remain firm. But what we do not realize is that each small denial trains us for a greater denial, so that if the time ever comes when a costly act of witness is demanded of us, we would likely fare no better than Peter. Then, by God's mercy, a dramatic reminder—such as the cock crowing in Peter's case—allows us to see how far we have strayed. The only way to train and be prepared for the most difficult decisions is to be faithful in the easier ones. And the opposite is also true: if we are not faithful in small matters, we will most likely fail also in the greater ones.

It is possible to deny Jesus in a number of ways; but not one of them is really acceptable. Whoever has an opportunity to witness and remains silent, denies Jesus. Whoever sees an injustice and ignores it, denies Jesus. Whoever is willing to bend the rules for a bit more income or for professional advancement, denies Jesus. Like Peter, most of us have denied Jesus repeatedly. And yet he still loves us!

Act: Pray: "My Lord and my God, there are so many ways I am tempted to deny my faith. There are many pressures in society. It is not always possible to 'get ahead' while remaining faithful to you. Give me insight, so that I may know when my faith and my witnessing are being threatened by the temptation to deny you, and give me the strength to remain firm. I pray in the name of Jesus, my Savior, who will never deny me. Amen."

Fourth Day: Read John 18:28-35.

See: John does not tell us what happened when Jesus was taken to Caiaphas. He simply says that after being taken to Caiaphas he was sent to the praetorium—the headquarters of Roman government. Once again, do not forget that Judea was part of the Roman Empire. The Romans allowed their subjected peoples a measure of autonomy and freedom, particularly in matters of religion. Thus, for instance, the Jews were allowed to have their Temple and their high priest, although the truth was that the Empire often used these institutions as a way to preserve order. At any rate, such local authorities could only function within certain limits. In this particular case, the religious leaders of Judea take Jesus to Pilate, because they are accusing him of a crime against the Empire—claiming to be King of the Jews—and also because they do not have the authority to condemn someone to death.

After reading this passage, one is struck by the religious scruples of these Judean leaders. They wish to retain their ritual purity, for Passover is approaching and they will not be able to perform their religious duties if they are defiled by entering the praetorium. This is sufficiently important to them that they force Pilate to come out of the praetorium to meet them and discuss their accusations. And yet, they are quite willing to bear false witness, which is clearly against their own Ten Commandments. Ritual purity is more important to them than moral purity.

Also striking is how vague the charges against Jesus are. When Pilate asks them about the charges against Jesus, all they can say is that he is a criminal, and that they have brought him to Pilate because they are not allowed to put someone to death. But apparently Pilate has some idea of the actual accusations against Jesus, for he takes Jesus into the praetorium—and therefore out of hearing of his accusers—and asks him if he is indeed the King of the Jews. A strange conversation ensues, in which each question is answered by yet another question. To Pilate's question, Jesus responds by asking if Pilate is asking the question on his own or whether someone has cued him. In other words, is he really following proper judicial procedure, or has he become a tool for the machinations of those who wish to destroy Jesus? Pilate answers with two questions: "I am not a Jew, am I?" and "What have you done?" In other words, I do not really understand what is taking place among you Jews; tell me why these people are accusing you.

Judge: Once again, we are struck by the contrast between the religious scruples of these Judean leaders, who do not wish to enter the praetorium and be defiled, and their lack of moral scruples, for they bear false witness against Jesus. Or perhaps they have convinced themselves that what they were saying was true, which is the most common way we often overcome situations in which we do not wish to act according to our own principles. This had been a continual concern of the ancient prophets of Israel, who repeatedly warned the people against the tendency to place religious rituals and observances above justice and truth. These Judean leaders are sincere, and their sincere religious convictions keep them from entering the praetorium; but they still follow an agenda—a religious agenda—that leads them to twist the Law to fit their convenience.

Again, we are not to think that this is something that happened only to those Judean leaders. The same has happened repeatedly throughout the history of the church. When the first conquistadores reached the Western Hemisphere, some of them insisted on having the native women baptized before raping them, so as not to be "mismatched with unbelievers" (2 Corinthians 6:14). Though they may not go to such extremes, we all know of people who insist on the literal inerrancy of every word in the Bible, and then discriminate against others for racist reasons. Others take up the banner of "Christian values" and promote their agendas through political and legislative processes, but refuse to use their political power to promote the cause of the homeless, or to provide medical services for the poor, or to prevent and criticize the misuse of military might. All of these examples point to the insidiousness of a sort of religiosity that believes that God can be served without practicing love and justice for all.

What about us? Do we believe that our service to God is completed once we have attended church, or once we have given our tithes, or once we have studied the Bible? Are there needs in the world that God is calling us to meet?

Act: Resolve that you will find ways to promote the discussion of these matters by the leaders and members of your congregation. Encourage them to ask: What can our church do to show that God is not interested only in religious matters, but also in the entire life of our community?

Fifth Day: Read John 18:36-40.

See: The dialogue between Jesus and Pilate seems to end with a question that Pilate poses: "What is truth?" Pilate does not wait for an answer, which seems to indicate that this is a rhetorical question. If so, what Pilate probably means to suggest is that there is no such a thing as truth, for facts can be bent according to people's convenience. At any rate, Pilate goes out again to discuss matters with the Judean leaders who have remained outside the praetorium. He reports his findings to them and issues a senseless verdict, for he contradicts himself. On the one hand, he tells them that he finds no crime in Jesus. On the basis of these words, it would seem that there is no reason to condemn Jesus, and Pilate should simply let him go. On the other hand, Pilate tells these Judean leaders that, if they wish, he will free Jesus, implying that he is also ready to punish him if they so desire. He tells them that he is ready to free a prisoner for Passover and seems to hope that they will choose Jesus. Clearly, he is trying to shift responsibility from himself to the Judean leaders, just as they have done with him earlier. But they will not let him off the hook so easily and ask that Barabbas be freed instead.

John explains that Barabbas was "a bandit." This was the name most commonly given to people who took off to the hills to carry a sort of guerrilla war against the Romans. Thus, it is quite possible that, as far as Roman interests were concerned, the crimes of Barabbas were greater than those of Jesus.

Judge: Both Pontius Pilate and the Judean leadership use Jesus for their own ends. Both wish to be rid of Jesus, but want to do it in such a way that the responsibility for his death will not be theirs. Obviously, there is still an underlying uneasiness about what they are doing; and therefore, while they know the outcome they seek, they would much rather have someone else be responsible for it. Both deal falsely with Jesus, not by lying to him, but by lying to themselves and to each other.

Given such a setting, Pilate's question, "What is truth?" turns out to be pointedly ironic. He is not really posing this question expecting Jesus or anyone else to answer it. What he means by it is that truth is unattainable, or at least that he is not really concerned over it.

For the Judean leadership, acting according to the truth would have required, not only that they remain undefiled for the celebration of Passover, but also that they remain undefiled by not bearing false witness. For Pilate, to speak the truth would have implied declaring openly and firmly what he in fact said, but did not defend: that Jesus was not guilty of the crimes for which he stood accused. Yet neither Pilate nor the Judean leaders spoke the truth, nor did they act according to the truth. They simply hid behind unspoken excuses and false legalism to attain their ends.

It is precisely at this point that the narrative becomes particularly relevant for us. It is quite easy to read the text and to blame Pontius Pilate or the Judean leadership. Indeed, in recent times there has been much discussion about how much responsibility the Romans bore, and how much the Judeans bore. But in following that path, we are actually evading what the text means for us, and not responding to the truth that confronts us in Jesus. If for those Judean leaders to "do the truth" would have implied not bearing false witness against Jesus, what might it mean for us today?

To do what is true means facing it without evasions. Jesus confronted Pontius Pilate as well as his other accusers. Jesus confronts us today, calling us first of all to follow him in discipleship. We try to evade this by claiming other priorities, by asking a thousand unimportant questions, and even by going to church and studying the Bible while doing nothing about it. In the end, Jesus is still there, confronting us with his answer: "I am the truth."

Once we have decided to be his disciples, Jesus still confronts us with the challenge of truth. There is much that is false in today's world. There is, for instance, the myth that anyone who is willing to work can find employment, and the myth that poor people simply don't care about their health or about the education of their children, and many other such myths. To allow such notions to circulate without challenging them and without trying to correct the evil behind them is to "wash our hands" of responsibility like Pontius Pilate. Wherever a child of God is abused, wherever this creation of God is destroyed, there is falsehood. To not oppose it is to share in it.

Act: Write on your notebook: "Falsehood, I know you." Now look at things and situations around you, trying to identify where there is such falsehood. Write down a few lines unmasking the untruths you see. Remember that untruth is not only hypocrisy and lies. It is also injustice, hate, and anything else that opposes the truth of God and God's love.

Upon completing your list, write on your notebook: *Falsehood, wherever I see you I'll unmask you.* Pray, asking for wisdom and strength to do what you have just written.

Sixth Day: Read John 19:1-3.

See: Pilate has just declared that he finds no crime in Jesus. But now, even in spite of such a declaration, he has him flogged. Pontius Pilate himself is an enigmatic figure. He was "procurator" of the Roman province of Judea from the year A.D. 26 to 36; but little is known of his life before or after. There are some ancient writers that tell us of his time in Judea and of the history of the province under his rule. Apparently he was a cruel man who enjoyed humiliating the Jews. Along those lines, we are told that the Roman governor of Syria, Vitelius, had to restrain him, so that he would not offend the Jews to the point of provoking a rebellion.

Given what is known of Pontius Pilate, one may surmise that he had Jesus flogged for two reasons. The first reason would be because of his own cruelty, his enjoyment of the suffering of others. The other would be his intention of humiliating the Judeans.

From the Roman point of view, being flogged was a very serious humiliation—so much so, that it was said that the very first of all the laws of Rome was the one that made it illegal to flog a Roman citizen. While the Judean leaders wished to have Pilate crucify Jesus, Pilate also takes the opportunity to humiliate all Jews through this one who supposedly was considered by some "the King of the Jews."

The Roman soldiers then join Pilate's cruelty and desire to humiliate. Remember that we are still in the praetorium, where the Judeans have refused to enter out of religious scruples. Therefore, all those present are Romans—except for Jesus. The soldiers mock Jesus, and in so doing, they are also mocking the entire Jewish nation, its dreams, and its religion. They put on him two symbols of royalty, a crown of thorns and a robe of purple. The symbolism of the crown needs no further explanation. As for the robe, the dye that was used for purple was obtained from tiny mollusks, and the very laboriousness of the process made the dye very expensive, to the point that it soon became a mark of royalty, or at least of high aristocracy.

Thus, what is happening within the praetorium while the Judean leaders wait outside is one of those acts of mockery of a culture or a tradition that are so common where different cultures meet.

Judge: Have you ever been in a situation where others have laughed at you or ridiculed you because of your race or culture? Unfortunately, the vast majority of people today belong to cultures or traditions or races that others mock and ridicule as inferior. In our own society, ethnic jokes abound. These are jokes in which people are stereotyped, and for the most part, are a way for those who share the joke to feel superior to those who are the brunt of the joke. In a way, this is what the Roman soldiers were doing by mocking Jesus. They were actually ridiculing the Jewish religion, and the hopes and expectations of the Jewish nation. Significantly, they were ridiculing even those who were their allies in the plot to destroy Jesus—the Judean religious leadership. And you will remember that Judeans did the same with Galilean Jews, whom they considered inferior.

When we say that Jesus came to undo the power of sin and for this reason he suffered the consequences of sin, we often forget that racism and feelings of racial or cultural superiority are consequences of sin. Jesus suffered for many reasons; but among them was the feeling of superiority Romans had toward Judeans, and Judeans toward Galileans. The Romans had become masters of much of the world, and they were convinced that this was because they were somehow superior to the rest—which is a very common reaction of the powerful seeking to justify their power.

What these Roman soldiers did not know is that in condemning Jesus they were condemning themselves. Their supposed civilizing superiority of which they were so proud, and which was the reason for their ridiculing others, was shown to be little more than barbarism clothed in power. The same is true of any supposed superiority that ridicules others and treats them as inferior.

Act: Discuss these matters with others in your church and community. Are there some who feel that they suffer discrimination? Are there some who are convinced that they are justified in discriminating against others or in ridiculing them? Have you ever been part of one group or the other—or both? Resolve never to say something about a particular culture, race, or tradition that you would not say in the presence of people belonging to it.

Seventh Day: Read John 19:4-11.

See: After all these acts of mockery, Pilate still wishes to let Jesus go. It is one thing to ridicule someone; killing them is another. Pilate was not so naive as to not know that Jesus had a following. The very fact that some of the Judean leaders accused him of trying to become the King of the Jews was an indication that he had a measure of popularity among Jews in general. To kill this man could easily result in riots, which the Roman military would eventually quench, but which would also be a bad mark on Pilate's political career.

Actually, this is what happened just a few years later. There was a rebellion among the Galileans and the Samaritans, and Pontius Pilate resorted to force in order to end it. When he learned what had happened, the governor of Syria, Vitelius, accused Pilate of having provoked the revolt by his poor administration, and Pilate had to return to Rome to render an account of his actions. Although we don't know what the outcome was, it is clear at least that Pilate was removed from his position of authority over Judea.

All of this was at stake at the trial of Jesus. This was why Pilate hesitated and tried to persuade the Judean leadership to let Jesus go. They would not be persuaded, but on the contrary, applied greater pressure on Pilate, who eventually did as they wished.

Judge: As we study the trial of Jesus, we have to deal with a subject rarely discussed in church: the power structures in society and how they affect Christian living. Sometimes we do discuss our responsibility for those who are not in the church, and we talk both about their need for the gospel and about their physical needs. But we rarely discuss how, in the world in which we live, people relate to each other along certain power structures, and how this affects our Christian responsibility.

When we speak of power, we tend to think mostly of those who are directly in power above us. If it is a matter of economic power, perhaps we think of the president of the bank who holds the mortgage on our home. If it is a matter of political power, we immediately think of the president and of some influential senators and others. If it is a matter of ecclesiastical power, we think of bishops and other leaders. But the fact of the matter is that all of these people who seem so powerful from our perspective are actually bound by an entire network of relationships—just as Pontius Pilate, who seemed so powerful in Jerusalem, was not so great in Rome. Knowing these circumstances, the Judean leaders apply pressure on Pilate by subtly suggesting that there are others above him and that he had better do what they desire. To this day, this is an important element in politics: knowing the interests, fears, and ambitions of the other players and using them to achieve a certain end.

Because we usually do not think in those terms, quite often we do not even understand what is taking place around us. We do not understand, for instance, why a mayor who had promised one thing eventually does another, or why the opinion of some people seems to carry more weight than the opinions of the rest. By telling the story of the trial of Jesus as he does, John is pointing to these complex power structures and inviting us to the difficult task of trying to discern how to be faithful in such a world.

Act: Consider again some of the problems and needs in your neighborhood you identified in previous weeks, as you reflect on how you and your church could serve your community. Try to draw a diagram sketching the structures of power and responsibility. For instance, if it is a matter of housing and you thought perhaps the mayor could solve it, place the mayor above the people in your diagram. But then think about who or what helps determine the mayor's actions. Add to your diagram elements such as "political party," "banks," "governor," "the press."

Now think about a strategy to achieve what you believe has to be done—in this case, providing better housing for the poor—using these various elements in such a way that the mayor or whoever is responsible will act as they should.

For Group Study

Lead the group in the exercise just described. Try to develop a concrete strategy. Invite the group to commit to it. If the group seems ready, help your project begin by distributing specific responsibilities among group members.

W E E K
TWELVE

First Day: Read John 19:12-16.

See: The "trial" of Jesus continues. In Pilate's very movements, John depicts him as a hesitant person, unsure of himself, constantly going in and out of the praetorium, and giving the Judean leaders a role they should not have had in a Roman trial. He goes in and out, talking with Jesus then with the priests several different times.

We finally learn the outcome of the proceedings. The Judean leaders are aware that Pilate is considering letting Jesus go, and they clearly threaten him with the possibility that the emperor will hear of the matter: "If you release this man, you are no friend of the emperor. Everyone who claims to be a king sets himself against the emperor."

Pilate comes out of the praetorium one last time, bringing Jesus with him, and with apparent sarcasm says to the Judean leaders, "Here is your King!" He may well be mocking, not only Jesus, but also the priests of Judea, whom this one man can so perturb. They do not seem to hear the sarcasm in his words, but simply insist that Jesus must be crucified. Pilate carries the charade on step further, "Should I crucify your King?" and they respond, "We have no king but the emperor."

At this point, Pilate finally agrees to the crucifixion and hands Jesus over to "them." It is not clear who "they" are. The context would seem to indicate that Pilate handed Jesus over to his Judean enemies. But crucifixion was a Roman, not Jewish, punishment. In tomorrow's passage, it will be "they" who crucify Jesus, but eventually, in verse 23, we will be told clearly that it was the Roman soldiers who actually crucified him.

Judge: The attitude of the religious leaders of Jerusalem is shameful, not only because they are committing a grave injustice, but also because they are using the power of their foreign oppressors against one of their own. After all, Jesus is also a Jew—though he may be a despised Galilean. Even though they do not agree with all his teachings and may deplore his deeds and his claims, he shares with them the same history and the same faith of Israel. He is a child of Abraham, just as much as they are. But their enmity toward Jesus is such that they seem to forget that it is the Roman Empire that has deprived them of their freedom, and they use that empire to rid themselves of Jesus. Significantly, the religious leaders of a nation that at times had prided itself for having no other king than God, find themselves declaring that they have no other king than the emperor.

This has been a constant temptation for believers throughout the ages. As early as the very first century, Paul had to admonish the Corinthians because they were rushing to take their disagreements to the civil courts, thus using those courts to punish those with whom they disagreed (1 Corinthians 6:1-8). After the Roman Empire declared itself Christian, and particularly during the Middle Ages, the Inquisition turned those whom it considered heretics to "the civil arm" to be executed, and were thus able to claim that the church was not killing anybody.

Today, we may not go as far as the Inquisition. But still there are Christians who will use whatever means are available to marginalize, shame, and even destroy those with whom they do not agree—much as those Judean leaders used Pilate and the power of the Empire to destroy Jesus.

Act: Make a list of those in your congregation or denomination with whom you most strongly disagree. Review your dealings with them. Have you always been charitable, understanding, and forgiving? If not, plan to approach those persons and make amends. Have you used inappropriate means—gossip, pressure, half truths, technicalities—to prevail over them? If so, pray for forgiveness and a more charitable spirit. Again, resolve to approach those persons and make amends.

Second Day: Read John 19:17-22.

See: We finally come to the crucifixion. John employs very few words to tell us about the greatest event of all the ages. In verse 17 he summarizes the long trek of Jesus carrying his cross to Golgotha, and in the next verse he says quite tersely: "There they crucified him, and with him two others, one on either side, with Jesus between them." The brevity itself adds to the poignancy of these words.

John then adds quite a bit about the inscription or sign on the cross, put there by Pilate's order: "Jesus of Nazareth, the King of the Jews." The inscription was written in the three languages that were then most common in the area—Latin, Greek, and what the Jews called "Hebrew," which at that time was actually Aramaic.

The Judean leaders are not happy with that inscription, which seems to imply that they and their people have acquiesced to Jesus' claim to kingship. They are eager to make it clear that this was Jesus' claim, and that they had no part in it. Also, the sign itself has ironic overtones, for Pilate may well be mocking the Jews and their messianic hopes—and thus mocking the very Judean leaders who brought Jesus to him. Finally, as it stood, the sign might also make it appear that Pilate was putting down a real conspiracy against Rome by crucifying Jesus—an impression these Judeans wish to avoid.

Their protest is to no avail. Pilate, who earlier allowed them to have their say against Jesus, now affirms his Roman authority. They have no voice in the matter. What Rome's representative has written will stand, no matter what the Judean leadership says about it. After all, crucifixion itself is a Roman form of punishment, and Rome—and Rome alone—has the right to decide how it is to be conducted.

Judge: It is often said that the Jews crucified Jesus. But this is not true. The truth is that it was the Roman authorities that crucified him, at the request and with the acquiescence of the Judean religious leadership. And even then, these Judean leaders were pushed aside when the time came to assert Roman authority.

The notion that Jesus was crucified by the Jews can perhaps be explained by events that occurred in the Roman Empire and in the Jewish nation after Jesus' death. After a series of rebellions shortly after the time of Jesus, the Jews were scattered over the earth, while the Roman Empire lasted for several centuries and eventually declared itself Christian. Once the Empire was Christian, it did not seem politic to accuse its authorities of having crucified Jesus. It was much more convenient to blame the Jews in general, and even to begin accusing them of "deicide," or killing God. A tragic result has been the long series of injustices committed by Christians against Jews through the centuries—while most tend to forget that it was actually the Romans who crucified Jesus. Almost incredibly, Christians seem to have forgotten that all the original disciples, and Jesus himself, were Jews!

History is often twisted to hide the evil and the mistakes of the powerful, and to hide the achievements of the powerless. We tend to give credit to leading figures and to ignore the many more who made significant contributions in quieter ways.

Act: Inquire about the history of your local congregation. Try to find out facts from different people. See if there is a group interested in recovering the history of your church—not just who the pastors were, but also who the lesser known members were, and how they contributed to what your church is today. If a group develops with similar interests, they may collect photos, letters, and other documents; they may ask some of the earlier members who are now advanced in age to record events that might otherwise be forgotten; they may communicate their findings to the rest of the congregation.

Third Day: Read John 19:23-30.

See: We are still at the scene of the crucifixion. Note that those who had crucified Jesus were "the soldiers"—that is, Roman soldiers. They were also the ones who took his tunic as loot and cast lots over it, after they had also divided the rest of his clothes among them. (It was customary in the Roman army to assign particular tasks, such as the custody of a prisoner, to groups of four soldiers. It was one of these task forces that crucified Jesus, and this is why there were four soldiers.)

Now John turns his attention to the only ones among all of Jesus' disciples, friends, and family who followed him to the foot of the cross: the women and "the disciple whom he loved"—most probably, John. From atop the cross, Jesus creates a new bond between his mother and this disciple: "Woman, here is your son," and to the disciple, "Here is your mother."

Jesus is then given sour wine. Finally Jesus declares, "It is finished," and dies.

Judge: Much could be said—and much *has* been said and written—about these few verses. Let us center our attention on what Jesus says to Mary and to John. This is a sign of his concern for his mother, who is losing her eldest son. But it is also more than that. These words from the cross remind us that in Christ new bonds are established—bonds that could be called family ties, but that go beyond the natural links within a family. The same Jesus who turns Mary and John into mother and son has turned all of us into brothers and sisters.

Those are titles we use quite frequently, and often glibly: "sister" and "brother." Sometimes when we say "Brother Brown," the very word "brother," rather than bringing us closer to him, has a distancing function—much as if we had said "Mr. Brown." Yet, if we take those words seriously, we shall see that they have far-reaching implications. In Jesus, we are all sisters and brothers.

This does not necessarily mean that we will like one another. Sometimes, in an earthly family, some members dislike others. I may not like an uncle or an aunt; but they are still my family. We did not choose them. We had no say about whether or not they would be part of our family. But they are, and we cannot change that. Likewise, in the family of faith, it is not us, but Jesus, who names our brothers and sisters. Through baptism we are grafted into this one family, into this one body of which we are all members—sisters and brothers. They are our family, not because we like them or because we get along well, but because they too are part of the family of God—a family not of our own choosing.

There are in our churches many people who do not have an immediate natural family, or whose family is far away. There are refugees from dictatorships, wars, and economic disasters. There are elderly people, most of whose relatives are dead. There are those who for whatever reason have been abandoned or rejected by their natural family. There are also those whose family life is fairly traditional and stable. How can the church be the family of God for all these different people?

Act: Give particular thought to people in your congregation who may be lonely or isolated. Spend some time with them. Think about how your congregation can be a family for people in your community who feel alone or abandoned. Discuss this with others.

Fourth Day: Read John 19:31-37.

See: John now turns to the events immediately after the crucifixion. Normally, people who were crucified were left hanging on the cross until they died—sometimes of asphyxiation, and sometimes of thirst and exposure—and even after their death, so that their rotting bodies would serve as a warning to others. In this case, since the coming Sabbath was a day of particular solemnity, the Judean religious leaders did not want the bodies hanging from crosses just outside the city, and therefore asked Pilate to have their legs broken and their bodies removed from the cross before the Sabbath. The purpose of breaking their legs is not entirely clear. Most likely, what would happen would be that these convicts, their legs broken, would be abandoned, and would die of thirst and starvation. In any case, remember that these Judean leaders refused to enter the house of Pilate, because they did not wish to be rendered unclean just before the festivities. It is for the same reason that they now ask that the convicts be removed from their crosses.

In compliance with this request, Roman soldiers are ordered by Pilate to break their legs and remove the convicts from their crosses. This they do with the other two convicts. But when they come to Jesus they find that he is dead. (Perhaps the soldier who pierces his side does so in order to make sure that he is indeed dead.) It is at this point that John tells us that blood and water flowed from Jesus' side. From a very early date, Christians saw in this combination of water and blood a sign of baptism (water) and communion (blood), both made powerful through the death and resurrection of Jesus.

Judge: Consider the deep religious commitment of those who sought to have Jesus crucified. There is here a terrible irony. It was precisely the religious leaders of Judea who conspired to have Jesus killed. Yet they would not enter Pilate's praetorium for religious scruples, and once Jesus has been crucified they are the ones who ask that he be removed from the cross. The reason for this request is not compassion toward Jesus and his family; it is simply that they are eager to go ahead with their religious observances, and to do so in as proper a way as possible.

Furthermore, John never says or even hints that these were insincere religious people. On the contrary, as they conspired against Jesus they were convinced that they were serving Israel and preserving its freedom to practice its religion. This is a constant temptation for religious people—Christians as well as others. We are so concerned over our observances and our rules that we easily forget their true meaning. When this happens, even if we are convinced that we are being faithful, we may well be opposing the will of God.

Concrete examples abound. A prosperous church with a magnificent building in the heart of a city decides not to allow its facilities to be used to shelter the homeless. They argue that these buildings have been erected for the glory of God, and that they would be profaned by sheltering people who have not bathed in a long time and who would bring trash into the facilities. In another church there is a raging debate because someone dared move the communion table. Whenever communion is celebrated, people scowl at each other. In an entire denomination, people have taken sides over a burning issue, and they now publish papers and pamphlets insulting each other and use Scripture as an arsenal of weapons against each other.

In each of these cases, how are we different from those Judean religious leaders who managed to have Jesus crucified, yet sought to fulfill their religious obligations by staying in Pilate's courtyard, and by having the convicts removed from their crosses? Sincerity is not enough. The will must also surrender to God, who will turn it to love.

Act: Pray: "Help me, Lord, distinguish between a destructive and hateful religiosity, and the true service you desire from your people. Keep me from hypocrisy, God of truth. Keep me from hatred, God of love. Keep me from committing injustice, God of justice. In the name of Jesus Christ, your loving and just Truth made flesh. Amen."

Fifth Day: Read John 19:38-42.

See: Two high-ranking Judeans, who were secret followers of Jesus, Joseph of Arimathea and Nicodemus, took care of the burial. Joseph requested and got permission from Pilate to bury Jesus. This is not surprising, for apparently all Pilate wished was to be rid of the entire matter and to antagonize as few of the Judean leaders as possible.

Nicodemus, for his part, brought a large amount of a mixture of myrrh and aloes, to anoint the body. This was customary among people of abundant resources, for myrrh was relatively expensive.

Joseph and Nicodemus then wrapped the body, as was customary, and buried Jesus in a tomb that was available. At that time, such tombs were usually a cave or an excavation in the rock, which was then covered with a large stone and sealed.

Judge: Remember that according to Jewish religious practice, corpses were unclean, and whoever touched a corpse was rendered unclean also. Thus, the charitable act on the part of Nicodemus and Joseph of Arimathea would defile them and prevent them from celebrating the coming feast with the rest of society. They would even have to keep apart from their families and friends until they were purified—and by then the feast would have passed. If their action became known—as it must—in the wider society, they would be regarded as irreligious people by the rest of the community. Yet these two—including Nicodemus, who had a high position in the synagogue—dare brave the scorn of their neighbors and friends to give Jesus proper burial. From the point of view of religious people at the time, what Joseph and Nicodemus did was not very religious.

Next Sunday, on our way to church, we will probably pass many people who apparently do not have the slightest idea of the importance of that day. If the weather is good, some will be on their way to the beach or to a family outing in a park. Others will be mowing their lawns. Some will simply be basking in the sun. It is very easy to condemn them. To be so careless, after all that Jesus has done for them! But, are we supposed to condemn and reject them? Can we somehow show them the love of Christ in us?

Suppose that a neighbor who is not very religious becomes ill, and there is no one available to take care of him or her on Sunday morning. Would you offer to stay away from church to care for him or her? What should you do?

Act: Repeat yesterday's prayer. If possible, discuss your reflections with others.

Sixth Day: Read John 20:1-2.

See: The text begins by telling us that these events took place "early on the first day of the week." The reason why is that from a very early date Christians began gathering for worship on the first day of the week (Sunday) to celebrate the resurrection of their Lord.

The main character in these two verses is Mary Magdalene. Much has been said and written about Mary Magdalene—most of it with no basis on Scripture. To the popular mind, Mary Magdalene was a prostitute, or at least a woman of loose morals, whom Jesus forgave, and who then followed this Master who offered her an understanding that society would not. She is often confused with the woman caught in adultery in John 8 or with the sinful woman who washed the feet of Jesus with her tears (Luke 7:36-50).

All of this is false. The passage in all the New Testament that refers to Mary Magdalene in most detail is Luke 8:1-3, where we are told about a group of women followers of Jesus. These women were not poor, for they covered the expenses of the group—at least, this is what seems to be implied in Luke 8:3, where we are told that these women "provided for them out of their resources." Thus Mary Magdalene, far from being a converted street woman, may well have been a rather well-to-do woman, one who had the resources necessary to lead an independent life, to follow Jesus, and to help support the entire group of disciples.

It is true that according to the witness of the New Testament, Jesus had healed Mary Magdalene of "seven demons"; but these are not necessarily demons of immorality. They may well refer to any of many diseases that were described as demonic at the time.

Mary came from Magdala, a town by the Sea of Galilee that was famous for its fisheries and its production of salted fish. She was therefore a Galilean, like the majority of the disciples of Jesus, and she had followed him from Galilee to Jerusalem—along with several other women. Then, when all the male disciples, except one, fled and hid, Mary Magdalene was one of those who remained at the foot of the cross.

Now we see her come to the tomb early in the morning. There she finds that the stone that sealed the entrance has been moved. Her reaction is to run to the other disciples and tell them that the body of Jesus has been stolen.

Judge: The reference to "the first day of the week" is important. Remember that, according to Genesis, God made the world in six days, and then rested on the seventh. Therefore, the first day of the week is a symbol or remembrance of the very beginning of creation. The first day of the week is the day of the resurrection of our Lord. It is the beginning, not only of a new week, but also of a new creation! As a reminder of this, some of the most ancient Christian baptismal fonts are octagonal: their eight sides are a symbol of the seven days of creation and the first day of the new creation—a new creation which the person being baptized is joining.

So, it is before dawn on the first day of the week that Mary Madgalene goes to her Lord's tomb. She must have been sad and tearful, for the Lord who healed her from the seven demons that held her—whatever they were—and whom she has followed all the way from Galilee, is now dead. Not only is he dead, but he has also suffered the shameful death of a convicted criminal, abandoned by most of his friends and followers. Now Mary goes to the tomb, perhaps as a last farewell before returning to Galilee and trying to pick up the pieces of her life.

She reaches the tomb, and suddenly realizes that someone has moved the stone that should be covering the entrance. She has the opportunity of being the first witness to the resurrection—an opportunity that she will have again and will then seize. But instead of receiving the joy of the miracle, she runs away, even more disconsolate than before, believing that the body of Jesus has been stolen. She has no idea what has been done to him. As if the last few days had not held enough pain and vindictiveness!

Judge: It is easy to feel superior to Mary of Magdala, who upon seeing the tomb open, did not imagine that perhaps her Lord had risen, and quickly came to the conclusion that the body had been stolen. But the truth is that we too have difficulty seeing and celebrating God's most wonderful deeds.

In a way, since that day when Mary went to the tomb, the entire church lives on "the first day of the week"—on the day of the resurrection of its Lord. We live at the dawning of a new creation, and we await its consummation. If we only look around with the eyes of faith, we will see miracles aplenty. We shall see God shaping a new creation. We shall see the hand of God taking the dust of a sinner and reshaping it, blowing upon it the breath of new life, as in that first creation. We shall hear the voice of God speaking over a confused or doubting believer, "let there be light." We shall see new light dawning over that and many other sinners—new light illuminating the world anew, opening new realities, sowing new dreams. Everywhere we look we shall see empty tombs from which people who were dead in their sins have arisen. We shall see a new dawn, the beginning of a new week, the birth of a new creation.

But too often that is not what we see. We are so enwrapped in our own concerns that we cannot see God's actions all around us. If we see an empty tomb, instead of rejoicing in the miracle, all we can think of is that someone has committed a sacrilege.

No matter how dark the night, it is the dawning of a new creation, the first day of the week, the day of resurrection! Let us celebrate it with faith, and everywhere we shall see God's creative hand and a world full of empty tombs pointing to the new day that will dawn.

Act: Review the events of last week. Where has God been acting in them? Think not only of your own life, but also of the lives of others, and of national and world events. There is no doubt you will see much darkness. But do you also see the light of early morning? Pray that God will let you see some of the signs of the new creation around you. Then write a prayer of gratitude for those signs of the new creation you can see right now. Try to mention some specific signs. Consider the possibility of telling others about this, perhaps in a gathering in church.

Seventh Day: Read John 20:3-10.

See: Peter and "the other disciple"—perhaps John—run to the tomb. The text does not say whether they are moved by hope or by fear. We who know the end of the story tend to read the passage as if Peter and the other disciple were running to see the miracle of the empty tomb. But the way the narrative progresses, neither we nor Peter and the other disciple are supposed to know of the resurrection yet. They run simply because Mary has brought them strange news, and they want to see for themselves.

The other disciple—apparently younger than Peter—outruns his companion, reaching the tomb first. He peeks in, but does not enter the tomb, waiting for Peter. Peter himself is more impulsive. He just runs into the tomb, and there finds the wrapping in which Jesus was buried, but no body. At this point the other disciple follows Peter into the tomb, and the text says that he believed.

The passage then goes on to explain, "as yet they did not understand the Scripture, that he must rise from the dead." This seems to be an explanation about why Peter had not believed the moment he entered the tomb.

Leaving the tomb, the two disciples returned. The NRSV says that they returned "to their homes"; but the text can also be understood in the sense that they returned to the other disciples—which would seem to make more sense.

Judge: In the story of the two disciples we see two different responses to the empty tomb. We are told that Peter entered the tomb, and that he saw what the other disciple (John?) also saw; but not a word is said about his believing anything as the result of what he saw. By contrast, the other disciple believed the moment he saw the empty tomb and the wrappings lying there.

Sometimes we imagine that, were we to witness an overwhelming miracle, we would really believe. But the fact is that true faith does not require miracles, and that any miracle, no matter how great, can always be explained away by those who do not believe.

Up to this point in the narrative, three people have seen the empty tomb. One of them, Mary Magdalene, thought that somebody had stolen the body of Jesus. We are not told what Peter thought; but we are not told that he believed. It was the third one, the "other disciple," who upon seeing the same things that the others saw, believed.

It may be that in some cases people come to believe because they have witnessed a miracle. But it is also true that the very act of perceiving the miracle is a sign of faith. To claim that, if we were given a really great miracle, then we would really believe is simply an excuse for our present unbelief—and for our present disobedience.

The main reason for lack of faith is a lack of commitment or a fear of commitment. In the rest of the narrative we will see that there were some among the disciples who were very much afraid. Perhaps Mary Magdalene does not dare believe because she has already had enough letdowns, and does not wish to face the possibility of one more. Peter denied the Master three times; and now, before coming to affirm his resurrection, he needs to be absolutely sure. For all of us, to have faith and to act on the basis of faith involves commitment and risk.

We know, for instance, that if we really have faith we will have to reevaluate and reorganize how we employ our time. And, since we are not really willing to do that, we block faith out. We know that if we had more faith we would have to modify our finances—perhaps both what we do with our money and how we make our money—and since we are not really ready to do that we block faith out. Then, as an excuse, we convince ourselves that the problem is that we have not seen a convincing miracle. But the truth is that we do not believe because we do not wish to believe; and we do not wish to believe because we are not ready to commit ourselves.

Act: Now that we are coming to the end of these "three months with John," it is a good time to move from study to commitment. Take your notebook. Review what you have written on it, particularly any resolutions or plans. Have you fulfilled them?

Write: "I am afraid of having more faith because in that case I would have to _____."

Complete the sentence. Pray for more faith. Consider the possibility of doing precisely what you have just written on your notebook.

For Group Study

Before the session, ask three people to prepare to play the roles of Mary Magdalene, Peter, and "the other disciple." Have them sit in the middle of the classroom and discuss what each of them saw, and how they reacted.

Once these three people have had a conversation among themselves, open the circle to include the rest of the group, and engage them in a conversation about why it is that we have or do not have faith.

WEEK
THIRTEEN

First Day: Read John 20:11-18.

See: We are back with Mary Magdalene, of whom we had heard no more after she ran to give Peter and "the other disciple" the news of the disappearance of the body of Jesus. She now returns to the empty tomb. Since Peter and the other disciple ran to the tomb, and after finding it empty returned to the other disciples, it would seem that Mary Magdalene, somewhat slower than the other two, arrived back at the tomb after they had gone. At any rate, there is no further conversation between Mary and them.

Now she is crying by the tomb. Apparently she cries both for the death of Jesus and for the disappearance of his body. Finally she looks into the tomb, and there she sees two angels dressed in white. This does not necessarily mean two winged creatures, as in the popular images of angels. It means rather that they are messengers from God. They ask Mary why she weeps, and she tells them that she is weeping because they have taken her Lord away, and she does not know what they have done with him—"they" meaning someone unknown to her.

It is at this point that she notices that there is someone standing by her and, thinking that it is the gardener, asks him if he has taken the body away. Jesus then calls her by name, and she finally recognizes him.

The phrase that the NRSV correctly translates as "do not hold on to me" has traditionally been translated as "do not touch me"—or, in a Latin phrase that has inspired many a painting, *nolle me tangere*. On this basis, some interpreters have thought that Jesus does not want to be touched because his body is somewhat ethereal. But the actual meaning is made clear in the

NRSV, "do not hold on to me, because I have not yet ascended to the Father." This is not a time for holding on to his body, but rather to go and tell the other disciples that he lives. The passage ends with Mary going to take the good news to the disciples that Jesus has risen from the dead, and that he goes to the Father.

Judge: If the good news of the gospel is that Jesus has overcome the power of death, that he is with the Father, and that there he awaits us in order to make us participants in his victory, John tells us that the very first person ever commissioned to preach the gospel was Mary Magdalene. Before Jesus commissioned her, Peter and the other disciple had seen the empty tomb and had gone to tell the others about it. But all they had seen was an empty tomb—where Mary also had preceded them—and, although John believed, what Peter thought is not altogether clear. Mary was the first person commissioned to carry the good news; and commissioned by Jesus himself. This clearly contradicts all the arguments and prejudices of those who think that only men should be allowed to proclaim the gospel.

Where do you think such prejudices have their roots? Can you imagine how much the church has lost through the ages, by not allowing women to employ all their talents and abilities?

Act: If you are a woman, consider the possibility that God may be calling you to new forms of ministry. If you are a man, write down a list of things you can do to support the ministry of women. No matter whether you are a man or a woman, look around you, to the rest of the church, considering the possibility that God may be calling a woman whom you know to the ordained ministry or to some other form of Christian service. If you think that you know such a person, pray for her. If at some time you come to the conviction that you should raise the issue with her, do so.

Second Day: Read John 20:19-23.

See: We are still in that wonderful day, the first day of the week, the day of the resurrection of the Lord. The disciples are gathered at a place that John does not specify, although it may well have been the same upper room where they had celebrated their last supper with Jesus and where, according to other texts in the New Testament, the disciples continued gathering.

At any rate, they had closed the door "for fear of the Jews." Remember that the disciples themselves were Jews. Therefore, those whom they fear are not the Jews in general, but the same Judean religious leaders who plotted Jesus' death. One can well imagine that the priests and members of the Temple guard would now wish to make sure that Jesus' movement does not continue, and that for this reason the disciples feared them and closed the doors against them.

But closed doors are no obstacle for the risen Lord, who now appears in their midst and greets them: "Peace be with you." His body still bears the marks of the cross, which he now shows to his disciples. (The text does not say why he does this—whether as proof that he has indeed suffered and risen again, or for some other reason.)

Then Jesus commissions these disciples: "As the Father sent me, so I send you." Since that commission is no easy task, but one requiring special power, Jesus tells them, "Receive the Holy Spirit," giving them authority to forgive or not to forgive sins.

Judge: Much could be said about this passage. Note that it begins with the disciples fearfully meeting behind closed doors and ends with a commission ordering them to go out. To allow them to do this, they will have the Holy Spirit.

Too often Christians and churches close themselves up within their own buildings, or within their own communities. This does not happen only when we literally lock the doors, but also in many other ways. For instance, sometimes we try to make sure that in church we do not discuss the issues that are being debated in the world, because we are afraid that they may cause unnecessary friction and divisions. Or, we decide not to take a risk in service to the community for fear of criticism. Or we gather always with the same small circle of friends, never opening our circle to those who could bring different perspectives or challenges. In all such cases, we are like those first disciples who fearfully closed the doors to their meeting place.

But the truth is that when Jesus comes to us, he both brings peace and sends us out into a mission that may well be difficult. He sends us as he was sent; that is, to a world where his disciples may well be crucified, and where they will certainly be criticized and opposed. Jesus sends us as he was sent; that is, to preach, to heal, to shake up those who are too comfortable with a religion requiring no commitment to the neighbor—and if necessary, to give our lives for others. This is certainly more than any of us can bear or do. This is why we are given the Holy Spirit. Sometimes we think that the purpose of the gift of the Spirit is that we may rejoice, or that we may boast about what we have received; but in truth the Holy Spirit is given so that we may go where Jesus went and do as he did.

Act: Discuss with other members of your church, and particularly with its leadership, what is the mission of your local church in the particular setting in which it exists. If your church has a "mission statement," study it, trying to discover ways your church can go out into the community, sent by Jesus in the power of the Spirit, to do as Jesus would have us do.

Write down your reflections. Continue this conversation within your community of faith, until you see results.

Third Day: Read John 20:24-31.

See: Here again we find Thomas, "the Twin" (*Didymus* in Greek). We saw him earlier as the daring disciple who, when Jesus decided to return to Judea in spite of the dangers lurking there, told the rest that they should all go with Jesus, even at the risk of their lives. Now we see him in a different episode that has marked his image through the centuries as the doubting disciple.

We are told that Thomas was not present when Jesus first appeared among his disciples. Therefore, his doubt does not make him particularly incredulous. He simply had not seen what the others had seen, and therefore told them that he required more proof than their word. In a rather hyperbolic statement, he says that he will not believe until he puts his finger in the mark of the nails and his hand in Jesus' side.

Now, "a week later"—that is, the next Sunday—the disciples are gathered again. Once again the doors are closed. And once again Jesus stands in their midst and greets them: "Peace be with you."

He then tells Thomas to go ahead and do exactly what he said he needed to do before believing: put his hand in the wound in Jesus' side. But Thomas does not really need such proof, and instead of insisting on his unbelief exclaims: "My Lord and my God!" To this Jesus answers with a general word that seems addressed to those of us who would come later: "Blessed are those who have not seen and yet have come to believe."

The passage ends with a note from the Gospel writer stating that there is much more that he could have said, but that he has already given sufficient grounds so that readers may come to believe and have life in the name of Jesus.

Judge: Here we once again encounter the theme, frequent in the Gospel of John, of the relationship between faith and proof. Jesus is sufficiently merciful to appear before Thomas and undo his doubt. At the same time, however, he also declares that those who did not see and yet believe are blessed.

We commonly think that those who are constantly speaking of the wonders they have seen, of an extraordinary act on God's part, of miraculous healings and the like, have more faith than the rest of us. But sometimes the truth may be quite different. Perhaps these are people who will only believe if they have constant proofs. If that is the case, miracles and visions, rather than pointing to our extraordinary faith, are signs of a tottering faith. Those who have faith do not require miracles in order to believe.

On the other hand, it is also true that those who have faith are able to see miracles that others cannot see. We already dealt with this a few days ago, but it is important to insist upon it. Those who have faith are able to see God's hand in much that those who do not believe attribute to chance or to mere natural causes.

Finally, remember that faith is not belief in miracles or in the evangelist who prays for a miracle. Faith is always faith in Jesus Christ, and in the Father, and in the Holy Spirit. It is faith in God. It is not faith in ourselves or even faith in our own faith.

Act: Pray: "I believe, Lord; help my unbelief. I believe, Lord; help my unbelief. I believe, Lord; help my unbelief. Amen." Throughout the day, repeat this prayer as often as you can. Tomorrow, at the beginning of your study session, write down the result.

Fourth Day: Read John 21:1-14.

See: We now come to the last appearance of the risen Lord in the Gospel of John. We shall study it for three days. The place is the Sea of Galilee, near the city of Tiberias, which John has mentioned before. Although we are not told when or how, the disciples (or at least these seven) have returned to Galilee and to their fishing.

Apparently these disciples who earlier left their nets behind in order to follow Jesus, and did so through the long period leading to the events in Jerusalem, have decided to return to their routine. As in many other cases, it is Peter who leads the rest: "I am going fishing." The other six follow and join him, and they all spend the night fishing, but catch nothing.

Then Jesus comes to them incognito, first asking them for food and then telling them to cast the net on the right side of the boat. The catch is amazing, and it is "the beloved disciple" who then first recognizes Jesus. Peter, impetuous as ever, jumps into the sea in order to reach his master sooner, while the rest follow with the boat, the net, and their catch. When they all finally gather on the seashore, Jesus becomes the host of the meal.

Judge: Although at first it may not seem so, in a way, the beginning of this story is one of the saddest passages in the entire Gospel of John. These disciples have seen their master crucified and risen. The Lord has commissioned them, sending them as he was sent. He has also given them of his Spirit so that they may fulfill that commission. What do they do? They go back to fishing near Tiberias, as if nothing had happened.

Going back to a routine may well be a sad sign of lack of faith. After the events of that Easter Sunday, to go back to fishing as if nothing had happened is almost insulting to the memory of Jesus and a denial of the Spirit he gave them.

Now that we are coming to the end of these "three months with John," if our lives have not changed in the least, if we have not made new commitments, if we are not ready for a fuller commitment, we are very much like those early disciples, who simply returned to their boats, their nets, and their fishing.

Sometimes we may be given signs that this is precisely what we are doing. These seven disciples caught nothing. Sometimes the routine that earlier seemed so good and productive loses its interest. We go days, weeks, and months "catching nothing"— finding little value in what we are doing. If that is the case, it may be time to cast our nets elsewhere, and see if the Lord is calling us to something out of our normal routine where we find ourselves so much at home, and yet unsatisfied.

Act: Two days ago you were invited to look around your community of faith for signs that Jesus might be calling someone in your congregation to the pastoral ministry or to some other form of ministry. Now it is time to look at yourself. God is calling you to ministry. There is no doubt of that. God calls all believers to ministry. The question is, to what sort of ministry is Jesus calling you? Is it what you are now doing? Is it something else? Write down your reflections. Pray about it. Discuss it with others in the church.

Fifth Day: Read John 21:15-19.

See: Yesterday's scene continues. Jesus and the disciples are still by the lake, where they have finished their supper. Three times, Jesus asks Peter if he loves him. In a way, this is an opportunity for Peter to reaffirm his love for Jesus as many times as he denied him a few days before.

It is clear, however, that love for Jesus has to go beyond mere words. This is why the dialogue leads to the call and commandment, "follow me." Given the entire passage, Jesus' call to follow implies at least two things. It implies, first of all, loving him and tending his sheep. Remember that very early in the Gospel of John we are told that Jesus is the Lamb of God. Later, Jesus says that he is the Good Shepherd. Now he speaks of his followers as both sheep and those who tend the flock. Thus, those who have become the flock of the Good Shepherd are also to be shepherds of the rest of the flock. Second, when Jesus tells Peter "follow me," he is literally inviting Peter to take his cross. Note that this call to follow comes immediately after the very serious words by which he tells Peter that he too, like Jesus, will die at the hands of others, being taken where he does not wish to go. Following Jesus means that the time will come when Peter will no longer be master of his own life, just as Jesus had to give up his life on the cross. "When you grow old, you will stretch out your hand, and someone else will fasten a belt around you and take you where you do not wish to go."

Judge: Following Jesus means first of all tending to his sheep. One cannot be a follower of Jesus on one's own. Following Jesus means caring for others who are also part of his flock, and who like us are engaged in the difficult task of confronting the forces of evil and proclaiming the hope of God's future.

Sadly, too often we Christians allow ourselves to be lured into a private sort of religiosity. Some people go to church by watching a service on television—not because they are shut-ins, but simply because they would rather hear a sermon in private than going out and gathering with a congregation. In this sort of Christianity, one expects to be fed constantly, but does little by way of feeding others.

The problem is that the Christian faith is such that in feeding others we ourselves are fed. Thus, if I stay at home listening to a famous preacher, I shall be spiritually undernourished—no matter how good the preacher may be. We have to join with other sheep who, like us, need feeding and caring. There is where Jesus leads when he says, "follow me."

With those words, he also invites us to a total commitment—to the death if necessary. Once again, such commitment is not attained sitting at home watching television. It is attained by living out the gospel, witnessing to Jesus, and working for justice.

Act: Resolve that during the next twenty-four hours you will contact at least two other believers to share your faith, and thus be mutually nourished.

Sixth Day: Read John 21:20-24.

See: Jesus has begun walking, and is being followed by Peter, who looks back and sees that the "other disciple" whom this Gospel never mentions by name, and who may well be John, is also following. Peter's question is probably not one of jealousy, but refers rather to what Jesus has just told him about his own old age and death. He has just been told that he will have to face sufferings similar to those of Jesus. Now, seeing this other disciple following, he wishes to know if he too will have to face the same lot. Jesus' response is that Peter ought not to worry about the future of this other disciple. What he has to do is follow.

Scholars point out that in the early church there were rumors that Jesus had promised that John would not die before the return of his Master. (This tradition became so strong, that for centuries people claimed that they had seen the earth moving atop John's tomb in Ephesus, and that this was because John was still breathing under the soil.) Verse 23 deals with this supposed promise to John and rejects it.

Judge: Peter's concern is understandable. Jesus has just predicted his martyrdom, and he wishes to know what the future holds for the rest of the disciples, particularly John. The problem is that this sort of concern, rather than strengthening discipleship, weakens it. Our task is not to predict the future. We know that the future is in the hands of our Lord, and that should suffice. Our task is to be obedient in the present, so that when the future comes we shall be ready for it.

Sadly, there are believers and entire churches today whose main concern seems to be predicting the future, trying to discern the date of the return of Jesus, or claiming that they can somehow foretell what will happen next. Some books of this nature have become best sellers. This is not a recent development, for it has been a temptation throughout the life of the church.

Even though Jesus told his disciples that the time of his return was not a matter for them to learn, there have been hundreds of teachers, biblical interpreters, and supposed seers who thought that they had fixed the date of this return. All those dates are now past, and this entire endeavor has left nothing but a long history of idle curiosity, failed expectations, and obedience deferred.

Our concern should not be to find out how Sister Jane will die, or what will happen to Brother James, or whether young Susie will become a great woman. Our concern and our business is to help Sister Jane, Brother James, and young Susie to become obedient disciples.

Act: If you have ever been tempted to try to find out what the future holds for you, remind yourself that your future is in the hands of God, and that it could not be in better hands. Your main concern should not be to find out about the future. Your main concern should be to be obedient each and every day, both today and in the future. Write and then repeat a prayer committing yourself to obedience, and ask the Lord to lead you today into whatever he holds for your tomorrow.

Seventh Day: Read John 21:25.

See: The passage is quite brief—a single verse. In concluding the narrative, the author of this Gospel tells us that what is written here is just a fraction of the deeds of Jesus, and that those deeds are so many, it is impossible to write down all of them. This is expressed with the powerful image that the result would be so many books that they would not fit in the whole world.

Judge: We finally come to the end of our three months of studying the Gospel of John. But the book of John itself tells us that this is not all that could be known about Jesus. This is so for at last two reasons.

First, since at the very beginning John tells us that "through him all things were made," the deeds of the Word of God—the Word that was made flesh in Jesus—are so vast that all that has been done is somehow part of his deeds. When a scientist—even one who is not a believer—writes about the inner structure of atoms, she is writing about the work of this Word that was made flesh in Jesus. When a camera mounted on a rocket sends us pictures of Jupiter, we are again seeing part of the works of this eternal Word of God. When a month-old baby smiles, we witness once again the deeds of this Word.

Second, leaving aside these cosmic dimensions of the Word incarnate in Jesus Christ, John invites us to realize that the works of Jesus did not end with his resurrection and ascension. Jesus has continued working, acting, and speaking through his followers, whom he empowered with the Holy Spirit. Through his thousands and millions of disciples, Jesus has confronted dictators much more powerful that Pontius Pilate. He has built thousands of hospitals and healed millions. Every day he feeds crowds much larger than the one once gathered near Tiberias by the Sea of Galilee. He has built and run homes for orphans, for the elderly and for the homeless; and established schools and universities; movements for the abolition of slavery, for women's rights; and on, and on, and on.

John wrote twenty-one chapters about Jesus. The church has continued writing additional chapters, so that all of us are also part of the gospel of our Lord Jesus Christ—a gospel still being written until it pleases God to put an end to this age.

Act: Pray: "Thank you, Lord, for your gospel. Thanks for the book of John. Thanks, because my name is written in the Book of Life. Take my life, and with it write a few more lines—humble but loving lines—in the vast history of your deeds for us and for your entire creation. Amen and amen."

For Group Study

After discussing how Jesus has continued acting and still acts today, invite the group to evaluate the three months that have just been completed. In this evaluation, include not only the study itself, but also how it has affected their views and their lives. Invite them to consider the possibility of another study, to continue the discipline they have developed.